100 YEARS OF ICONIC

TOYS

ROADS Publishing
149 Lower Baggot Street
Dublin 2
Ireland

www.roads.co

First published 2016

1

TOYS

Designed in Ireland by WorkGroup
Print manufactured and managed by
Jellyfish Solutions

British Library Cataloguing in
Publication Data.
A catalogue record for this book is
available from the British Library.

978-1-909399-90-7

100 YEARS OF ICONIC

TOYS

ROADS

PUBLISHING

Introduction

In 2006, Lego launched a brand new advertising campaign. The concept was simple – an unassuming combination of bricks was placed against a coloured background. But the silhouette displayed something different – an airplane, a dinosaur, a ship. Another ad, dating from the 1980s, shows a young red-headed girl proudly presenting a jumble of blocks, and the tagline simply says: 'What it is is beautiful.' Each of these ads was meant to pluck at the same heartstring – the imagination of a child is more valuable than gold.

Walk down a Lego aisle today, however, and what will be most apparent is that ready-made 'sets' have replaced the free-for-all attitude of years gone by. No longer do children (and parents) have to imagine that randomly combined Lego blocks represent a spaceship – the work is done for them, with branded vehicles, weapons, props and characters making up the greater part of the sets. Now, it is rare for a TV or film franchise aimed at children to escape Lego-ification.

Something else that might catch your eye, strolling surreptitiously down the Lego aisle, is colour coding. Pinks, purples and pastels dominate some areas – here you will find princesses, castles, pets and stylish convertibles. Move over to the next aisle, and the next, and you'll begin to spot a trend. Girls' toys, it seems, only come in shades of garish fuchsia, while boys' toys are muted, earthy colours, depicting exciting, manly pursuits, such as race-car driving and exploration.

Do children's tastes in toys vary so much by gender? The classic Lego ad from the 1980s would suggest not, as would the majority of the iconic toys featured in this book. Take a look through its pages, and try to spot many explicitly gendered examples. With a few exceptions, the majority of the toys we cherish from our childhoods were remarkably 'equal opportunity'. Super Soaker fights didn't require a pink-versus-blue breakdown. Mr Frosty provided sticky and unwholesome frozen treats to all. Troll dolls are remarkably (and uncannily) genderless.

So what's the reasoning behind the pink–blue divide?

Instead of asking whether children's taste in toys varies by gender, the more appropriate question might be: do advertisers' tastes in markets vary? Back in the sixties, as G.I. Joe was strapping on his army camos for the first time, a decision was made, possibly over a glass of Scotch in some murky, smoke-filled *Mad Men*-style advertising firm. These new toys weren't dolls – oh no. They were *action figures*. And with that, from Thunderbirds to Teenage Mutant Ninja Turtles, boys around the world would be sure to tell you in no uncertain terms that 'dolls were for girls'. And so it was: two types of toy, two genders, two colours – and two markets.

While the watershed moment may not have been as dramatic and immediate as that, it is true that toys today are more divided along gender lines than fifty years ago. Whether or not this is simply a result of clever marketing, this trend seems to be reversing itself, with various campaigns such as 'Let Toys Be Toys' gaining momentum online, arguing that instilling gender stereotypes into children at a young age is unnecessary and damaging. In 2012, Hasbro, after an online petition gained much traction and publicity, announced they were releasing a silver, gender-neutral model of the Easy Bake Oven. And in 2015, a Barbie commercial featured a young boy for the first time.

It's hard to overstate the role advertising has had in shaping our perception of the toy market. Everyone remembers a catchy jingle from a childhood advert, and the fact that most people can still reel off one or two advertising hooks from decades ago says a lot.

Mr. Potato Head was one of the first toys ever to appear on TV sets, in 1952, and the first to appeal directly to children. Some credit him with unleashing the phenomenon of 'pester power' – the 'I-want-it-I-want-it-I-want-it' refrain that is so familiar to parents. Funnily enough, the original Mr. Potato Head didn't come with a plastic body. Children had to supply their own potato (or other root vegetable of their choice). This frivolous waste of food, however, did not go down well with the post-War generation, whose childhood had been one of privation, so a plastic potato was added to the kit in 1964.

Many of these early toys came about from the most serendipitous of events. For example, rubber shortages during the First World War led to the creation of Silly Putty. Play-Doh began life as a wall cleaner; it was used as a way to get soot marks off wallpaper – and with

the transition from coal-based stoves to natural gas, the company needed a new market for their product. The View-Master came into being thanks to the invention of Kodachrome colour film, making small photographic images easy to produce.

Toys have often acted as important signs of the times, and changes to their design reflect shifts in public consciousness. See, for example, the history of G.I. Joe, which provides an insight into attitudes towards the military in the United States. Originally, in 1964, Joe was the all-American soldier, designed to inspire pride in the fighting men of the Air Force, Navy and Armed Services. However, the advent of the Vietnam War, along with widespread disapproval of American foreign policy, led to a necessary redesign. Joe became an adventurer; an international hero that took on supervillains and jungles rather than an unspecified foreign threat.

The sixties also led to the advent of 'fads' – the all-encompassing, got-to-have-it mentality that can lead to riots, black-market deals, broken hearts and empty wallets. Hula Hoops and Twister were two of the biggest crazes during this period, and it is perhaps no coincidence that they are both tied up with the free-flowing, sexually liberated popular image of the Swinging Sixties. Twister was even derided as 'sex in a box' by its critics.

Pop-culture icons began to creep into the toy world during the seventies. Evel Knievel, daredevil extraordinaire and the cause of thousands of copycat broken bones, became immortalised in a line of action figures that allowed children to put Evel through his paces in their own homes. The release of the first *Star Wars* movie in 1977 caused mass hysteria, and the toy line that followed it is as collectable now as it was in the seventies. A mint condition Millennium Falcon can still change hands for hundreds of dollars, and for many, the knee-high AT-AT is the holy grail of collectables.

The eighties brought the world many toy lines that are still surviving to this day. Both Transformers and Teenage Mutant Ninja Turtles have received the Hollywood treatment in recent years, with massive, live-action blockbusters hitting the cinema screens, complete with explosions, action sequences and obligatory love stories. My Little Pony has bounded back into the public consciousness, with the *Friendship is Magic* series attracting a whole new audience: 'bronies' – older, male

internet dwellers who obsess over the antics of Twilight Sparkle, Rainbow Dash, Pinkie Pie and Applejack. It was acceptable in the eighties, it seems, and it's still acceptable now.

The rise of technology dominated the nineties. Game Boys were the hottest property, not necessarily because of the advanced computing power, but rather the fact that it was the first truly portable console – a toy, in essence. Kevin McCallister's antics in *Home Alone 2* sent a generation out to stores to pick up a Talkboy, keen to start new and exciting careers as international spies, all with the help of this fairly basic tape recorder. Tamagotchis and Furbies, as addictive as they were bewildering, provided parents with an easy alternative to a real-life pet – although many found themselves regretting this decision when it became apparent that incessant beeping and garbled 'Furbish' were just as irritating as a chewed slipper.

Post-2000, innovative and must-have toys have become rarer. Possibly due to the abundance of options on the market, riot-inciting toys such as Tickle Me Elmo are unusual, but a number of interesting exceptions stand out. Bratz, Barbie's younger, trash-talking sisters, became the subject of some controversy upon their release. Alongside a hefty

intellectual property lawsuit, parents worried at the oversexualised example the doll line was setting.

In recent years, there has been something of a revolt, with dolls like Lottie receiving much publicity. Lottie has childlike proportions, dresses age-appropriately, and engages in wholesome and educational activities such as stargazing and fossil-hunting. In another positive step forward, in August 2016 the Toy Industry Association announced that it would be dropping gendered categories for its 2017 Toy of the Year Awards.

Vive la Révolution.

When we set out to put this book together, we consulted lists, articles, magazines, books and experts – we overturned every stone to make sure we were including toys that were iconic, game-changing or unique in some way. After that, we cast the net as wide as possible. We went to our friends, family members, colleagues, strangers in the street – we asked them all the same question: What do you remember?

And the answers came hard and fast, and each one came with a story. One staff member recounted a still-fervent belief that Alien Eggs were to come alive at the turn of the Millennium. Another reminisced about their favourite 'hunk' from Dream Phone. Yet another cautiously admitted that Mastermind tournaments were still a common Friday-night activity in her house. Our photographer chipped in with his own recollections, and proved a point by correcting us when we referred to a Thunderbird as a doll – 'It's not a doll, it's an action figure.' Everywhere we looked, there were stories and memories popping out of the woodwork.

Gathering the toys proved to be its own challenge. Some, we bought new, and these will be donated to charity. Others, long out of production, we had to beg, borrow and steal. While some

people were delighted to have their toys included, we hadn't reckoned with the separation anxiety that comes with parting with a vintage AT-AT or a treasured collection of Pokémon cards.

The more modern toys were a challenge in another way, but we wanted to be sure to include toys that reflect post-millennial changes in the market. Rainbow Loom, for example, was met with head-scratching, but one staff member displayed a hitherto unseen talent for bracelet-making, and whipped up a couple of examples. Squinkies were another unknown quantity, but we soon learned that these tiny figurines had become popular at the height of the recession, and their wallet-friendly size was a huge part of their popularity.

All in all, what we've learned is that toys become popular for a reason; reasons that are often intrinsically tied up with the historical and cultural situations of the time. In that way, toys provide a fascinating insight into history – and into our own personal memories.

Right now, nostalgia has become a fad in itself. Reboots are everywhere. Hollywood has run out of ideas, and every toy franchise from decades past is being scoured to see if there is a secret blockbuster hiding in there. The past is fashionable again – whipping out a Game

Boy or He-Man figurine in polite company will incite jealousy and awe, rather than an uncomfortable silence.

We like to remember. Call it a regressive response to societal upheaval, a rose-tinted displacement technique, a yearning for simpler times, an irresponsible fancy, a response to responsibility, a symptom of the eventual downfall of society – we don't mind.

Because every one of us has, at some point, looked in distain at a modern child's game, and found ourselves thinking: We had better toys when we were young. It is at this point, generally, that despair sets in, and the existential angst of maturity becomes overwhelming.

But fear not! You hold the solution in your hands. In this book, we have collected the most iconic, popular, bizarre and downright dangerous toys that made up our childhoods. We're sure we've missed some, because in some ways, one hundred toys is not enough to tell the story of childhood itself. But we have tried.

So fire up your Talkboy, grab your Pound Puppy, let Teddy Ruxpin tell you a story, lock and load your Super Soaker and keep an eye out for rogue Sky Dancers. With this book, you can prove that yes, it's true: We had better toys when we were young.

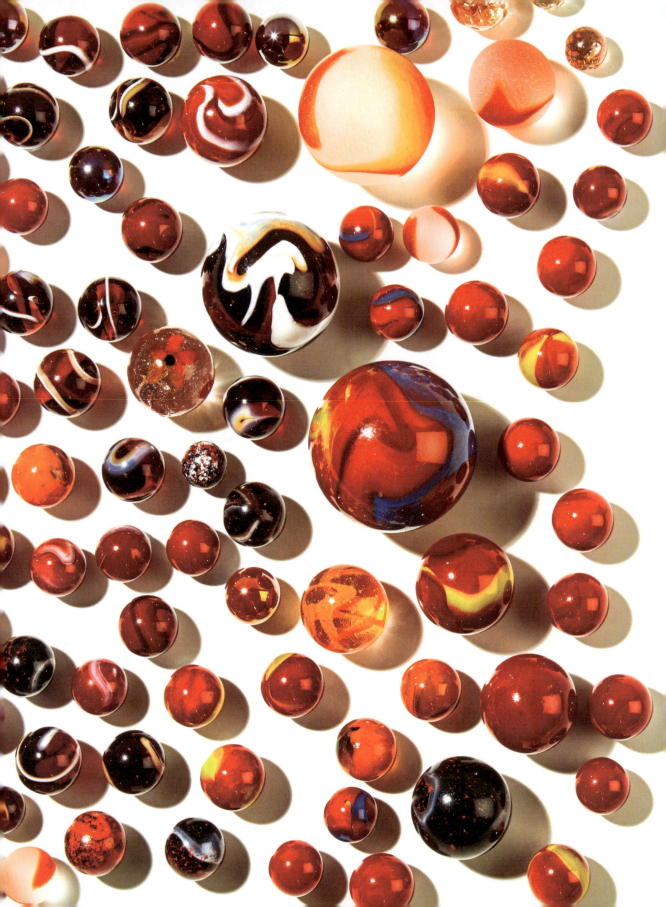

Marbles

1884

Marbles are one of the earliest forms of game play developed by humans. While the exact date of origin is unknown, artefacts have been found in Paleolithic caves in Austria, Ancient Egyptian sarcophagi and early Greek and Roman settlements, and there are mentions of nut games in Ovid's 'The Walnut Tree'. The appeal of the game spread across all classes, cultures and ages. Mass production of marbles began in 1884 with Sam Dyke of Akron, USA. He created a mould that allowed for the production of up to 1 million marbles per day. This reduced the cost of the toy considerably and allowed marbles to become far more accessible. While traditionally considered a children's game, adults often amass huge collections of rare and unusual marbles. Marble playing is still a popular pastime and has a large vocabulary of accompanying slang. A whole language has developed around the game and the aesthetic of the marbles themselves.

The British and World Marbles Championship has taken place in Tinsley Green, West Sussex, England, since 1932. The marble-playing season begins on Ash Wednesday annually and ends on Good Friday, as it was thought that playing after then was bad luck.

Meccano

1901

Amateur engineer Frank Hornby came up with the idea of a child-orientated construction set in 1901. First known as Mechanics Made Easy, it was registered as Meccano in 1907. The kits included perforated metal strips, gears, pulleys and axles, and nuts and bolts were used to connect them. The pieces came in a tin box, along with instructions for twelve different builds.

In response to demand, a new factory was constructed in Liverpool in 1914 to manufacture the elements on-site. The unique appeal of the toy lay in the fact that the same pieces could be used to create a number of different designs. Hornby also launched the Meccano Guild in 1919 and founded the *Meccano Magazine*, which ran from 1916 to 1981. Meccano is still popular today, with additions such as electric motors enhancing the creative potential of the system.

In 2009, English television presenter James May, along with a team of engineers, created a twenty-three-metre bridge over the Leeds and Liverpool Canal using Meccano. Four years later, May created a Meccano motorcycle and successfully rode it across the Isle of Man.

Teddy Bear

1902

Everyone remembers their first teddy bear and few toys conjure such strong attachments as they do. Despite being a timeless object of love and affection, the invention of the teddy bear has a grisly origin. In 1902, while on a bear-hunting trip in Mississippi, former President of the United States Theodore 'Teddy' Roosevelt was invited to shoot a black bear that had been captured and beaten by the other hunters. He refused to shoot, deeming the act unsportsmanlike, and demanded that the bear be given mercy. A cartoon depicting the incident appeared in *The Washington Post*, showing Roosevelt defending an adorable bear cub. Seeing this cartoon, Morris Mitchom was moved to create a soft toy of the bear. He dubbed his creation 'Teddy's Bear' and went on to found the Ideal Novelty and Toy Company. Transcending trends in children's toys, the teddy bear remains a favourite all over the world.

Two teddy bears accompanied aviators Alcock and Brown when they made the first non-stop transatlantic flight in 1919.

Crayola

1903

The Crayola brand has its origins in a Pennsylvanian industrial pigment supply company, whose founders identified the market for safe, affordable wax crayons for children and adults. The brand name derives from *craie*, the French for 'chalk', and 'ola', a then-popular shorthand for 'oily', and it was this combination that gave the crayons their unique smell, which still has the power to transport millions of adults back to their childhoods.

As the Crayola company grew, so did their range of colours, and they currently make 120 shades. In 1990, eight colours were retired to make way for new ones. Today, the public can visit one of the 'Crayola Experience' visitors centres in Easton, PA, Orlando, FL and Minneapolis, MN (with more locations to come throughout the US).

In 1996, the Crayola factory produced its 100 billionth crayon, and two years later, the Crayola crayon rightly became one of the first inductees to the newly inaugurated US National Toy Hall of Fame.

In 2000, Crayola asked the American people to vote for their favourite crayon colour; among the celebrity respondents, Britney Spears chose 'Robin's Egg Blue', Whoopi Goldberg picked 'Magenta', and George W. Bush swore his allegiance to 'Blue Bell'.

Kewpie Doll

1912

Kewpie dolls began life in 1909 in the comic strips of illustrator Rose O'Neill, as cartoonish characters that resembled baby cupids. They first appeared in the *Ladies' Home Journal*, and they were so popular that J.D. Kestner, a German toy company, agreed to manufacture 3D versions of the characters in 1912. The first Kewpie dolls came in nine sizes, were made from celluloid and bisque porcelain, and many of them were signed by O'Neill herself.

An immediate success, the doll was one of the first examples of a toy fad, and quickly became a household name. The characters began to appear everywhere, including on posters supporting women's suffrage. At the 1939 New York World's Fair, a time capsule was put into the earth to be uncovered in the year 6939. A Kewpie doll was included, alongside an almanac, a pack of Camel cigarettes, and a dollar's worth of change. Many of the early Kewpie dolls are today worth thousands of dollars to collectors.

In Japan, Kewpie is a popular brand of mayonnaise, and the bottles feature the dolls on the front.

Lincoln Logs

1916

Lincoln Logs were invented by John Lloyd Wright, son of the legendary architect Frank Lloyd Wright, in 1916. When the two were working on the construction of the 'earthquake-proof' Imperial Hotel in Tokyo, John noticed that his father's design made use of interlocking log beams to create a sturdy foundation. On his return to the United States, he developed a toy set with notched wooden logs that could be laid at right angles to create buildings, and was issued a patent in 1920.

The original sets came with instructions on how to build famous structures such as Uncle Tom's Cabin and Abraham Lincoln's childhood home. These nostalgic links, along with the name of the toy itself, invoked ideas of the frontier and the pioneering spirit of early settlers, and the toys became an immediate success in the rush of patriotic sentiment that followed the First World War. Lincoln Logs have remained an iconic childhood toy in the USA since then, and they were inducted into the Toy Hall of Fame in 1999.

The original Lincoln Logs packaging featured Abraham Lincoln alongside the slogan: 'Interesting playthings typifying the spirit of America.'

Hornby Trains

1920

Engineer Frank Hornby, creator of Meccano, launched his first toy train, a clockwork 0 gauge, in 1920. An immediate success, the first electric train was produced in 1925. In 1938, Hornby introduced their Duplo range, half the size of the 0 gauge, which became the industry standard for toy trains. Production faltered during the Second World War, and Hornby faced stiff competition in the 1950s, leading to the purchase of the company by Line Brothers in 1964.

The Hornby brand became independent again in 1980, and is now known simply as Hornby. Although originally intended for children, the detail and variation in the train sets led to huge collector interest. A number of organisations, such as the Hornby Railway Collectors' Association, continue to produce various publications and enjoy high membership rates today.

Inventor Frank Hornby also dabbled in politics and served as a Conservative MP from 1931 to 1934 in the Everton district of England.

Yo-yo

1928

The yo-yo has been in constant circulation as a toy since it was invented in Ancient Greece, circa 500 BC. Many variations have existed, but the fundamental principle remains the same: a circular two-disked axle with a string attached.

The concept enjoyed renewed popularity when Pedro Flores opened the Yo-yo Manufacturing Company in 1928. Following the success of the product, entrepreneur Donald F. Duncan released a redesigned version of the toy and in 1932 the name yo-yo became a registered trademark.

Today, the popularity of the yo-yo may have lost its momentum, but there are still many contests and events around the world where competitors display their yo-yo skills and prowess.

The name yo-yo is a relatively recent invention, with the toy having been dubbed the *bandalore*, *emigrette* and *joujou de Normandie* over the years.

Cap Gun

1930

Cap guns originated in the aftermath of the American Civil War, when firearm companies, who had enjoyed a number of booming years, were forced to diversify. In the 1930s advertisers identified the potential of marketing cap guns for role-playing games, and sales exploded in the late 1940s, with the popularity of Western television shows like *The Lone Ranger*. Sales soared after both World Wars, but slowed during the '60s and '70s, as images from Vietnam War brought home the realities of conflict.

Although they are not as widely available today, cap guns and other varieties of toy guns still sell in their millions in the USA, with research showing that sales are more common in rural areas in red states. Debate among experts continues on the effects, positive or negative, of these toys; some say they encourage violence, others that fantasy violence is helpful in understanding its weight in the real world.

In 1989 legislation was passed in the USA that demanded that toy guns have brightly coloured tips, due to the number of incidents where young people were shot by police officers who thought they were carrying real guns.

Army Men

1938

The production of these inexpensive American figurines began in the late 1930s. Standing at five centimetres in height, these military miniatures were portable and practically disposable. Originally made from metal, the advent of plastic in manufacturing meant that these little green men could be mass-produced and sold cheaply, while avoiding the hazards of lead-based materials. Ubiquitous in pop culture as the quintessential American boy's toy, the designs of the soldiers themselves reflected trends in wartime uniforms. The popularity of toy army men was subject to current opinion regarding war and violence; for example, during the Vietnam War, there was a distinct decline in production and sales of the minuscule military men.

Green army men appear frequently in the *Toy Story* franchise, where they work as a team under the direction of 'Sarge'.

Lego

1939

Lego bricks are one of the most creative and versatile toys of the twentieth century. Invented by carpenter Ole Kirk Christiansen in Bildung, Denmark, production began in 1939. The name Lego is derived from the Danish phrase *leg godt* meaning 'play well'. Each brick is meticulously designed and rigorously tested; Lego bricks are so structurally sound that it would take 375,000 bricks stacked on top of each other to make the bottom brick collapse. There are now six Legoland amusement parks and dozens of popular films and video games, and such is the cultural impact of Lego that it was among the first inductees into the National Toy Hall of Fame in 1999.

As part of the Lego Bricks in Space initiative, thirteen sets of the building blocks were brought to the International Space Station to demonstrate scientific concepts in microgravity.

Skipping Rope

1940

Evidence shows that skipping was enjoyed as early as 1600 BC in Ancient Egypt, Ancient China and by the Aborigines of Australia. Jumping rope became a popular pastime in America in the 1940s and 1950s; it is thought that some of the first rope jumpers in America were Dutch settlers, hence the term 'Double Dutch'. It evolved into an inner-city expression of movement and became highly stylised, involving breakdance and gymnastic elements. The game can be enjoyed solo or with many participants and varies in levels of skill and intricacy. Some of the techniques for solo jumpers include the easy jump, the alternate foot jump, criss-cross, side swing, double under, toad, leg over, Awesome Annie, inverse toad, elephant, frog kick, and the James Hirst. A large element of skipping is the accompanying rhymes; together they create a form of physical poetry, with the rhythmic patterns of the rhymes punctuated by the treading of feet hitting concrete.

The world record for the most skips in thirty seconds is 162.

Slinky

1943

The 'Official State Toy' of Pennsylvania was invented by Richard T. James in 1943. A naval mechanical engineer, James was stationed at the shipyard of William Cramp & Sons, a company that was developing springs that would stabilise instruments aboard ships in rough seas. He discovered the stepping properties of the springs accidentally when he knocked one from a shelf. Inspired by the strange movement, he set out to design a spring that had sufficient tension to walk. The toy became a sensation, with the first edition of four hundred units reportedly selling out in just ninety minutes. The jingle that accompanied the first advert is now the longest-running in history.

Avant-garde composer John Cage employed an amplified Slinky in his 1959 work 'Sounds of Venice'.

Silly Putty

1943

In 1943, engineer James Wright was attempting to create a synthetic rubber compound, as the Second World War had led to strict rationing of rubber products. By combining boric acid and silicone oil, Wright managed to create a gooey substance that would bounce, stretch, had a high melting point and was non-toxic. However, his new invention did not have the properties required to replace rubber, and so it was shelved for a number of years.

In 1949, Ruth Fallgatter and Peter Hodgson decided to market the bouncing putty in red plastic egg containers, and in 1950, at the International Toy Fair in New York, Silly Putty was introduced to the world. Advertisements on *The Howdy Doody Show* in 1957 would send the sales into orbit, and in 1968, the product went into space for real on board Apollo 8. Crayola acquired the rights to produce Silly Putty in 1977, and it was inducted into the National Toy Hall of Fame in 2001.

Originally, children could use Silly Putty to lift the type from newspapers. However, although the recipe of the putty remains the same, changes in the inking process mean that this is no longer possible.

Tonka Truck

1946

Mound Metalcraft, the company that originally manufactured Tonka Trucks, was set up after the Second World War as a garden-tool manufacturer. After testing steel diggers alongside their main products, they realised that the toys were the more marketable concept. The toy line expanded to forklifts, dump trucks, fire trucks, cement mixers and cranes, and the company changed its name to Tonka Toys in 1955. In 1965, Tonka released their most famous product, the Mighty Dump Truck, which was a bright yellow truck that was both realistic and sturdy, and it became a must-have for children everywhere.

Hasbro acquired the brand in 1991, and the line is now made up of thirty different trucks, which are generally made from plastic, although metal versions of the classics are available. Tonka Trucks were inducted into the US National Toy Hall of Fame in 2001.

Tonka advertised the durability of their Mighty Dump Truck with an advert in the 1970s that showed an elephant standing on the toy, unable to break it.

Subbuteo

1947

Creator Peter Adolph had a great love of falconry, so much so that when he could not name his game Hobby, he chose to name it after the hobby falcon, whose Latin name is *Falco Subbuteo*. Originally, the pitches were fashioned from old army blankets, which were to be found in virtually every home following the Second World War, and the game came with instructions on how to mark out the pitch with chalk. The game followed traditional football rules and its huge popularity led to the founding of the Table Soccer Players' Association. The 'flickable' figurines underwent many material changes, from cardboard to a heavyweight plastic figure. The 'heavyweight' figure was designed by Charles Stadden, and each player was assembled and hand-painted by housewives in Tunbridge Wells.

Subbuteo has left an indelible mark on generations, leading to numerous pop culture cameos: it is played in the Colin Firth film *Fever Pitch*, name-checked by The Undertones in their pop classic 'My Perfect Cousin', and an iconic black-and-white photograph from the 1990s shows Liam and Noel Gallagher of Oasis engaging in a brotherly game backstage before a show.

Cluedo

1949

Cluedo – or Clue, as it is known in North America – is a hugely successful and enduring murder-mystery game in which three to six players turn detective to identify a crime scene, a culprit and their weapon. Set in an English country house, the colourful cast of Miss Scarlett, Mrs White, Mrs Peacock, Professor Plum, Reverend Green and Colonel Mustard have gone on to feature in books, video games, a stage musical and in the 1985 film *Clue*, starring Tim Curry and Christopher Lloyd, which, although not a box-office success, has become something of a cult classic.

One of the most popular board games of all time, Cluedo has been produced in more than fifty countries and licensed to numerous pop-culture franchises, with The Simpsons, James Bond, and Harry Potter versions appearing on the shelves, introducing new audiences the world over to 'The Great Detective Game'.

Alongside the candlestick, revolver, lead pipe, rope, spanner, and dagger, the original game's weapons included an axe, poison, a bomb, a syringe and a shillelagh.

49

Fuzzy Felt

1950

During the Second World War, Lois Allan's outbuildings were used to manufacture felt gaskets for sealing tank components, and she was struck by how much the employees' children enjoyed playing with the felt offcuts, which they stuck to the reverse of table mats. Allan's first commercial sets, consisting of colourful shapes, were an instant success, and over time themed sets were introduced, including the circus and the farm, and later branded sets with popular characters like Noddy and Thomas the Tank Engine.

It was, and remains, an inexpensive toy that can generate hours of creative and quiet play – a distraction without the destruction. Since its release, more than 25 million Fuzzy Felt sets have been sold around the world. Sales have significantly declined since its peak in the 1970s, but many children of the seventies, now nostalgic adults, continue to purchase the sets for their children.

The backdrop to designer Stella McCartney's Spring/Summer 2009 collection was a 7 × 14 metre Fuzzy Felt collage featuring giraffes and rabbits by controversial British artists Jake and Dinos Chapman.

Mr. Potato Head

1952

The original toy featured plastic body parts and features that could be pushed into a potato or other vegetable, but post-Second World War sensibilities disapproved of this frivolous use of food. George Lerner struggled to find a toy company willing to produce his product, but Hassenfeld Brothers liked his idea so much that the name 'Mr. Potato Head' was thought up and the toy went into production in 1952.

The marketing of Mr. Potato Head revolutionised the industry, as it was the first toy to be advertised on television directly to children. Immediately successful, the toy launched the fledgling Hasbro Company into the annals of toy history.

Safety concerns surrounding the sharp spikes used to insert the pieces into vegetables lead to the addition of a hard plastic body in 1964. Other shapes such as carrots and cucumbers were briefly released in the 1960s, but the potato remained the definitive vegetable of choice.

Mr. Potato Head appeared in the 1995 Disney smash hit *Toy Story*, and its subsequent sequels, prompting a resurgence in popularity. In recent years, Hasbro has released themed versions to tie in with blockbuster releases, such as Darth Tater (*Star Wars*) and Optimash Prime (*Transformers*).

In 1985, Mr. Potato Head ran for the office of mayor of Boise, Idaho, and received four votes, which landed him a spot in *The Guinness Book of Records*.

Play-Doh

1956

Play-Doh originated as a wallpaper cleaner in the 1930s, as coal-based fires were common and a product to remove soot from the walls was in demand. However, in the 1950s, oil and gas heating became more widespread, and the company, Kutol Products, had to come up with a new way of producing revenue. After a family member used the wallpaper cleaner in the classroom to create Christmas decorations, the idea of marketing Play-Doh as a toy was born.

Non-toxic and non-staining, the product was perfect for children, and the company soon added colouring and began to sell Play-Doh in a metal tin. A marketing deal with the children's television show *Captain Kangaroo* increased the toy's popularity, and by the late 1950s, sales were through the roof.

Today, Play-Doh remains popular in classrooms and at home, and various accessories and moulds have been released to help children create their own personal masterpieces. The basic ingredients are flour, salt, water, boric acid and mineral oil, but the exact recipe is a closely guarded secret. Play-Doh was inducted into the Toy Hall of Fame in 1998.

In 2006, for Play-Doh's fiftieth anniversary, Demeter Fragrance Library released a limited-edition perfume based on the scent of fresh Play-Doh.

Frisbee

1957

Inventor Fred Morrison claims he first had the idea for a flying disc toy while tossing a cake pan around on a beach in 1937. Originally named the 'Flyin' Cake Pan', then the 'Pluto Platter', his first plastic prototype underwent many improvements before going on the market.

Upon selling the rights to the Wham-O toy company, the name 'Frisbee' was decided upon, based on the original Frisbie Pie Company whose lids had been used as a toy for years. Under the guidance of Ed Headrick and Wham-O, the design was perfected, sales skyrocketed, and the Frisbee fad was firmly established by 1959.

Sports such as ultimate Frisbee and Frisbee golf became entwined with the spirit of counterculture in the 1960s, with pioneer players such as Ken Westerfield helping to popularise them further. In 1985, the World Flying Disc Federation was formed to encompass all these fledgling sports and create a community to regulate international competitions.

Upon his death, Headrick was cremated and his ashes were moulded into a number of limited edition Frisbees. Iconic, instantly recognisable and ever-popular, the Frisbee was inducted into the Toy Hall of Fame in 1998.

Back to the Future Part III (1990), set in the Wild West of 1885, features Marty McFly seeing a Frisbie Pie Company lid and exclaiming 'Hey! Frisbee! Far out!'

Scalextric

1957

The forerunner to Scalextric was a range of popular clockwork cars known as Scalex, developed by a British company called Minimodels. Inventor Fred Francis began experimenting with electricity to further develop the product. By adding small motors to his cars and placing them on a battery-powered track, Francis created an electric racetrack that could be powered by means of small triggers. He named the new toy Scalextric, a portmanteau of 'Scalex' and 'electric', and it was launched in 1957.

Many of the toy cars are based on real racing vehicles from events such as Formula One, NASCAR and the Grand Prix. Film and television tie-ins have also been released, featuring vehicles and characters from the James Bond, Batman and Spiderman series. Today, the brand is owned by Hornby, and remains a popular racing set.

In 2009, a team led by British TV presenter James May created a 4.75-kilometre-long Scalextric track, breaking the Guinness World Record.

Hula Hoop

1958

While the plastic hula hoop that we know today has its origins in 1950s Los Angeles, children and adults have been using variations for thousands of years. Hoops made of natural materials such as willow branches, vines and bamboo were used in ancient Egypt for recreation, in Greece for exercise, and in fourteenth-century Britain for religious rituals.

Arthur Melin and Richard Knerr had established their company Wham-O in 1948, and when they put these plastic hoops into production they promoted the toy with giveaways and demonstrations in Californian playgrounds. It was a massive and immediate success, selling in vast numbers thanks to its low retail price of $1.98. It is estimated that 25 million hoops were sold in the first four months, and a total of 100 million in the first two years. Thereafter, sales slowed steadily but the hula hoop remains a ubiquitous product around the world, both for children and adults, with the latter group embracing hooping as an exercise activity. The hula hoop was inducted in to the USA's National Toy Hall of Fame in 1999.

The world record for hula hooping is held by Ohio man Aaron Hibbs; in October 2009 he kept the hoop spinning for a dizzying 74 hours and 54 minutes.

Troll Dolls

1959

Troll dolls, also known as Dam dolls, were first created in 1959 by Danish fisherman Thomas Dam. The story of the toy could have come straight out of a fairy tale: too poor to buy his daughter a Christmas gift, Dam carved the first Troll doll out of wood. When the dolls were noticed by other children, Dam made more and more, and the operation soon snowballed. The bizarre appearance of Troll dolls, inspired by Scandinavian folklore, added to their appeal. With colourful, outlandish hair and bright eyes, the Trolls were as weird as they were collectable.

By the 1960s, Troll dolls had reached the US. However, a copyrighting error meant that cheap replicas were everywhere, and it wasn't until 1994 that the trademark would be restored to the Dam family. After a lull, the 1990s saw a revival of the franchise, with spinoffs appearing out of the woodwork, including a 'Battle Trolls' line aimed at boys, a cartoon, a musical, accessories and numerous video games. In 2013, Dreamworks announced that it had purchased the rights to the line.

In 2016 MAC Cosmetics launched a super colourful make-up range in honour of Troll dolls, that included 'Bubble Butt' lip gloss, 'Suns Out Buns Out' eyeshadow and 'Dance Off Pants Off' lipstick.

Etch A Sketch

1960

The Etch A Sketch is one of the most iconic toys of all time, with more than 100 million sold since its release. Beginning its life as *L'Ecran Magique*, this incredibly creative toy was invented by French electrician André Cassagnes in the late 1950s. The toy made its debut to the world at the 1959 International Toy Fair in Nuremberg, Germany, and was released in the United States in time for Christmas 1960 by The Ohio Art Company under the new name, Etch A Sketch. The demand for the toy was so huge that the company had to maintain production until noon of Christmas Eve that year.

Challenging the user's dexterity and imagination, the Etch A Sketch works on the principle of static. Integrating aluminium powder beneath a glass screen, the two knobs control a moveable stylus that allows the user to create lines and images. To erase the image all the user has to do is to turn it upside down and shake. The Etch A Sketch featured in each of the *Toy Story* films and was inducted into the Toy Hall of Fame in 1998.

The 2012 United States presidential campaign had an unprecedented effect on the toy's sales when Mitt Romney's campaign advisor Eric Fehrnstrom compared Romney's politics to playing with an Etch A Sketch. The company reported a sales increase of 30 per cent and released an election-themed limited edition version in response.

Sophie the Giraffe

1961

Sophie's early birthdate (25 May 1961, the feast of St Sophie) might come as a surprise to some, but *Sophie la girafe* has been made in France for more than fifty years. Made from rubber derived from the sap of the Hevea tree, Sophie was the brainchild of Monsieur Rampeau, a French rotational moulding expert.

Sophie took off on the global market in 2002 after a French expatriate in the US contacted the manufacturer, Vulli, and requested permission to import the toy. After a number of high-profile endorsements from celebrities and parenting blogs, Sophie began to jump off the shelves. Described as an all-natural toy, with a flexible body and an eye-catching design, Sophie's soft shape appeals to parents and teething infants alike. In the midst of a Chinese toy recall, Sophie's eco-friendly build seemed a welcome relief from multisyllabic chemical compositions, and babies the world over agreed.

More Sophie the Giraffes are sold in France annually than babies are born.

Easy-Bake Oven

1963

The original Easy-Bake Oven was released by Kenner in 1963 as a working miniature oven that allowed children to cook alongside their parents. It made use of an ordinary light bulb as a heat source, came with pans and cake mix, and was sold under the advertising slogan of 'Bake your cake and eat it too!'

Perhaps due in part to the contemporary trend for fast, ready-made food, the Easy-Bake Oven was an immediate success, and became the must-have toy of 1963. The first design was a simple green or yellow oven, but it changed in colour and shape over the years, with models such as the 'Mod' being released in 1971 and a microwave version in 1981. In 2013, a black and silver design was released after a thirteen-year-old girl gathered over 40,000 petition signatures for a gender-neutral oven.

The Easy-Bake Oven was inducted into the Toy Hall of Fame in 2006, and in 2007 the original bulb was replaced with a greener dedicated heating element. In 2013, author Todd Coopee published a book named *Light Bulb Baking* to honour the fiftieth anniversary, which documents the history and influence of the toy.

In the TV show *Friends*, it is revealed that as a child, the character of Monica had six or seven Easy-Bake Ovens and a restaurant called Easy Monica's Bakery.

Mouse Trap

1963

The board game Mouse Trap was designed by Hank Kramer of Marvin Glass Associates and released by the Ideal Toy Company in 1963. The premise is similar to that of a Rube Goldberg machine – a contraption using interlinked everyday objects that set off a chain reaction to achieve a simple outcome. In this case, the objects include a boot, a bucket, a chute, a crank, a bathtub, a see-saw and a plastic diver. Players must roll dice to progress through the game, adding pieces to the machine. The end goal is to create the eponymous Mouse Trap and capture the other player's piece.

The correct sequence is described in a 1990 television commercial: 'Just turn the crank, and snap the plank, and boot the marble right down the chute, now watch it roll and hit the pole, and knock the ball in the rub-a-dub tub, which hits the man into the pan. The trap is set, here comes the net! Mouse trap, I guarantee, it's the craziest trap you'll ever see.'

According to a 2004 *Denver Post* article, Hank Kramer 'was a toy designer who couldn't stand children. Including his own.'

G.I. Joe

1964

A major design point of the first G.I. Joe was the use of articulated limbs, meaning that the figure could be posed in many different ways. The original toy was envisioned as a counterpoint to Barbie, to appeal to young boys; despite this, the word 'doll' was forbidden, with the creators instead preferring the term 'action figure'.

G.I. Joe has been hailed as an enduring figure of the American culture wars. When first released in the midst of the Cold War in 1964, he came in four incarnations, each a proud member of the different military branches – the Army, the Marines, the Navy and the Air Force.

However, as anti-war sentiment blossomed around the Vietnam War in the late sixties, demand for a militaristic children's toy declined, and Joe was remodelled in the seventies as an 'adventurer'. A relaunch in the eighties, combined with a successful marketing campaign and a smaller model, saw G.I. Joe reach new heights of popularity. Appearing in video games, comic books, TV cartoons and even a feature-length film, the range expanded to include a fictional team of villains known as COBRA.

Each episode of the 1985 TV series *G.I. Joe: A Real American Hero* ended with a public service announcement that attempted to teach children a moral message. These always ended with, 'Now you know, and knowing is half the battle.'

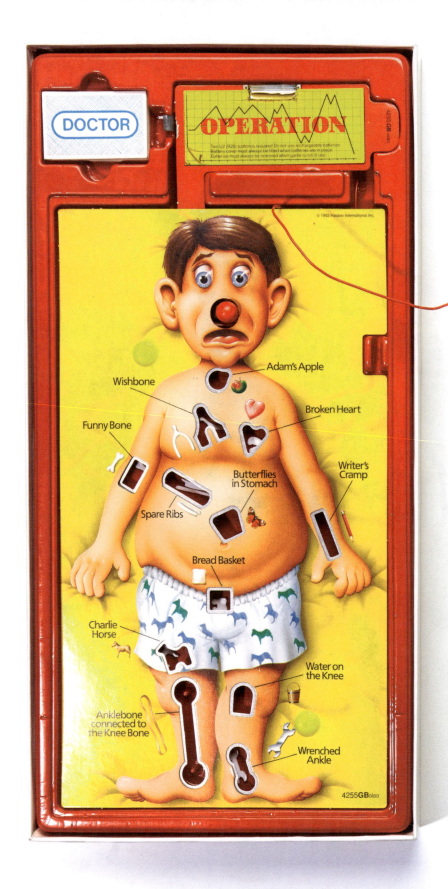

Operation

1964

Operation, an electronic, skill-based game that challenges the player to take on the role of doctor, was created by John Spinello, an industrial design student, and was licensed to Milton Bradley in 1965. The patient, an unfortunate known as 'Cavity Sam', has a number of ailments that can only be cured by the player carefully removing the afflicted part from the body with tweezers. However, if the player touches the side of the cavity, a buzzer will sound and Sam's nose will light up, passing the turn to the next player.

The original game required the player to remove individual body parts such as the 'Adam's Apple', 'Wrenched Ankle', and 'Funny Bone', along with treating more abstract ailments like 'Butterflies in Stomach'. In 2004, fans got the chance to vote for a new ailment, and 'Brain Freeze' was added to the game. Various versions have been released to tie in with cinema and television releases, but the original Cavity Sam remains as poorly and popular as ever.

In recent years, Sam's complaints have taken on a more modern twist, with 'Gamer's Thumb' and 'Headphone Headache' demanding the players' attention.

Barrel of Monkeys

1965

Leonard Marks came up with the original concept for Barrel of Monkeys while playing around with a number of metal chain links. A friend put him in contact with Milton Dinhofer, a successful toy importer, who, upon hearing Marks' initial concept, envisaged a toy made up of monkeys with linking arms. The game was originally known as Chimp to Chimp, and was renamed in 1965, when the idea was picked up by Lakeside Toys, after the common phrase 'more fun than a barrel of monkeys'.

The game is made up of a coloured plastic barrel and ten to twelve plastic monkeys, depending on the edition. The concept is simple – a player picks up a monkey and attempts to use the piece's arm to hook a second piece, and then a third. If the player drops any of their monkeys, the turn is passed to the next person. The player who creates the longest chain is the winner. In 2015, Barrel of Monkeys celebrated its fiftieth anniversary on the market.

A number of world records have been set using this game, including for speed runs and for the longest continuous chain of monkeys.

Thunderbirds

1965

Thunderbirds is a long-running British TV franchise focusing on the exploits of International Rescue, a team of heroes that operates out of the fictional Tracy Island. The primary cast is made up of Jeff Tracy and his sons Scott, Virgil, Alan, Gordon and John, each of whom pilots a different type of rescue vehicle. The original 1960s show made use of a type of electronic puppetry known as 'supermarionation', a term coined by producer Gerry Anderson.

The first Thunderbirds toys were die-cast, and produced by Dinky and Matchbox in the 1960s. A television revival in the 1990s led to the release of another set, and in 2000, Vivid Imaginations released a new range to coincide with yet another rerelease. The toy collections included each Thunderbird vehicle, a wide cast of characters, and a Tracy Island playset.

In 1992, due to a production shortage, demand for a Tracy Island model was so great that children's TV show *Blue Peter* ran a segment instructing children on how to make their own.

Twister

1965

In 1964, as part as an advertising campaign for shoe polish, Reyn Guyer conceived of a life-sized game that would use people as the playing pieces. When he showed 'King's Footsie' to his co-workers to great success, he was convinced he was on to a winner. With help from Charles Foley and Chuck Rabens, the game was developed further and was renamed 'Pretzel', then 'Twister', and it was acquired by Milton Bradley in 1965.

Initially, buyers were not convinced due to the risqué nature of the game, but when Johnny Carson and star Eva Gabor tried out Twister on the *Tonight Show* in 1966, its fate was sealed. The provocative nature of the game caused its competitors to denounce Twister as 'sex in a box', but the Swinging Sixties embraced the game with both hands, and it was named Game of the Year in 1967. Milton Bradley went on to advertise the game as fun for all the family, and since then Twister has remained a party mainstay all over the world.

The 1991 film *Bill & Ted's Bogus Journey* features the main characters challenging Death to a number of games in exchange for their lives — a parody of Ingmar Berman's *The Seventh Seal*. Eschewing the chess of the original, Bill and Ted choose modern games, and are finally allowed to leave hell after winning a tense game of Twister.

Spirograph

1966

The Spirograph was invented by British engineer Denys Fisher, whose firm had the impressive credentials of being previously employed by NATO. It was originally envisioned as a drafting tool for engineers, but Fisher was encouraged to market it as a toy. It was presented at the 1966 Nuremberg International Toy Fair and went on to win Toy of the Year the following year.

The Spirograph consists of a number of plastic gear wheels that can be used in different combinations. When the user pushes a wheel with a pen to rotate it, they can create geometric patterns. By alternating the wheel size and position, children could produce psychedelic designs that seem to tap into the spirit of the 1960s. The patterns were so popular that they even influenced the worlds of art and fashion design.

Digital simulations of the technique are now common, and are often used to explain mathematical principles to students. In 2015, the Spirograph celebrated its fiftieth anniversary with new releases and a die-cast collector's set.

The geometric shapes created by a Spirograph are mathematically known as hypocycloids and epicycloids, depending on where the second wheel is placed.

Lite-Brite

1967

Lite-Brite, an art toy created by inventor Burt Meyer, first came on the market in 1967. Meyer, who worked for toy designers Marvin Glass and Associates, then sold the idea to Hasbro. Children loved the creative possibilities offered by Lite-Brite, and it has remained in production ever since.

The toy makes use of a grid of holes and coloured pegs. Children would push the pegs through sheets of black paper to form patterns on the grid, which was then backlit by a simple lightbulb. The light was blocked by the black paper, and shone through the translucent coloured pegs to create a patterned display. The user could either make their own free-form images, or follow a pattern to create a particular design. Nowadays, Lite-Brite also appears as an app that can be used on smartphones, tablets and computers.

The Guinness World Record for the largest Lite-Brite picture ever created used 596,897 pegs and was created in Minnesota in 2013.

MiniTill

1968

For sixty-five years, English company Casdon has
specialised in toy replicas of everyday objects from
the home and high street, designed to help children
learn about daily life. Alongside cooking and cleaning
apparatus such as kettles and hoovers, Casdon
produces miniature sweetshops, post offices and
supermarket tills. These may seem unglamorous to the
touch-screen generation, but these toys enhance social
skills, hand-eye co-ordination and numeracy. Once
marketed as a luxury toy, the original MiniTill is a relic
of its time, with a distinctive colour scheme uncommon
(if not completely absent) in twenty-first-century toys.
Casdon have moved with the times, however; current
incarnations include a brightly coloured Chip 'n' PIN
till, and an interactive self-service checkout.

A redesign of the original till was
called for with the dawn of
decimalisation in 1971; ahead of the
curve, Casdon launched the revamped
version three years early, and it has
been suggested that the uncertainty
of the new system led to the unusual
organisation of the figures.

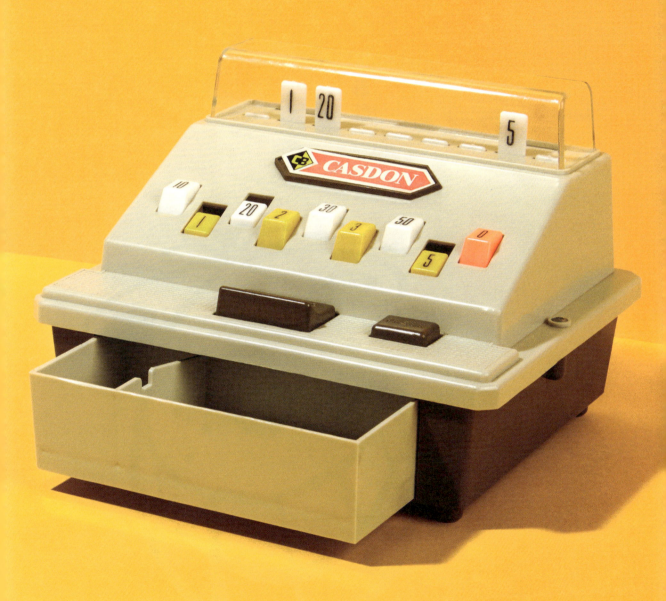

Space Hopper

1969

Known as a Space Hopper in the UK and a Hippity Hop in the USA, this toy was christened a Pon-Pon in its native Italy. Inventor Aquilino Cosani was inspired by a documentary about kangaroos, and he created a toy whose genius is in both its initial simplicity and its ultimate impracticality – the joy of bouncing is married to the hilarity of slow progress and often falling off.

While it is a slightly different version of the original, which had rigid handles, the Space Hopper we know today sports a very distinctive kangaroo face, which was used during UK production to test for leaks. The process of making a Space Hopper involves two moulds, one with horns, into which the molten PVC is poured. These are then joined and spun, coating the insides, and baked before adding the valve for inflation.

The first Space Hopper was produced in the UK in 1969 and its popularity skyrocketed in the 1970s, selling 200,000 per year at its peak and becoming one of the defining toys of that decade.

At time of printing, the record for the fastest mile on a space hopper is 13 minutes flat and was set by Ashrita Furman of New York on 19 August 2010.

Stickle Bricks

1969

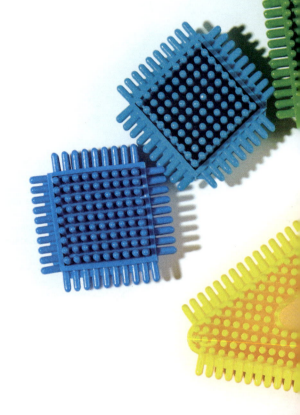

Created by inventor Denys Fisher in 1969, Stickle Bricks are a building toy intended for toddlers and younger children. The pieces consist of coloured plastic shapes with 'stickles' – thin plastic protrusions that can be used to link two or more pieces together. Children can create simple or complex structures, and the ease with which the creations can be broken down adds to the appeal of the toy.

A standard set contains square, circular and rectangular pieces, while more modern versions include accessories such as wheels, flowers and animals. While various versions of the toy exist, Hasbro are the current owners of Stickle Bricks, and they are produced by Flair Leisure Products.

With their bright colours and unique textures, Stickle Bricks appeal to children on multiple sensory levels, and are often used in various forms of child therapy.

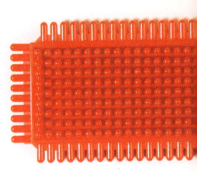

Pogo Bal

1969

Known by various names internationally, this toy was christened Springbal by its Belgian creators in 1969. It was named Pogo Bal by Hasbro when it launched in the US in the mid-1980s and became an immediate craze. Its composition is simple and durable – a figure-8 rubber ball surrounded by a platform of thick plastic – making it perfect for outdoor play. To use the Pogo Bal, you place your feet on the plastic ring, gripping the ball on either side, and hop. The accompanying US television advertisement featured gravity-defying teenagers bouncing effortlessly, but in reality, like its precursor the pogo stick and the Space Hopper, travelling with the Pogo Bal required significantly more energy than walking, and today it is a popular piece of exercise equipment, due to its effectiveness in developing a strong core.

In 1987, Pogo Bal was marketed as 'the hottest craze in America', with print ads declaring it the ultimate toy of the decade and inviting young people to 'Jump out of the 50s and into the 80s!'

Nerf

1969

Nerf is a soft toy brand that includes many forms of sports toys and foam-based weapons.

In 1969, Reyn Guyer approached Parker Brothers with an idea for a ball game that could be played indoors without damaging furniture or people. Nerf debuted the next year as a small foam ball made from polyurethane that was dubbed 'the world's first indoor ball'.

Following this success, the company began to release Nerf products in other forms, such as a Super Nerf Ball, the Nerfoop, and Nerf Ping Pong. However, it was their move into foam-based weaponry that cemented the brand as a must-have toy line. Today, most of the products are based around foam projectiles that are launched from a plastic weapon. Bows and arrows, traditional guns, crossbows, blasters and dart guns are all part of the range today.

In 2013, Nerf launched Rebelle, a series of weapons in pinks and purples that were marketed at girls and inspired by the popularity of the *Hunger Games* series.

Styling Head

1970

Styling Heads for professional hairdressers had been around for decades, but from the 1970s, similar models aimed at children began to gain popularity. Featuring long, style-able hair, accessories and make-up, young girls could play out their cosmetic fantasies on these doll busts. Gaining in popularity in the 1980s and '90s, versions were released with more and more accessories, with everything from temporary tattoos to hair dye appearing in kits. Some even featured 'growing' hair – tresses that could be lengthened or shortened at the turn of a wheel or the touch of a button. Many toy companies have released versions of the Styling Head, and popular children's characters from television and film have also been given the treatment.

Styling Heads often reflected the fashions of the time: dolls from the 1970s tended to sport long, loose curls, '80s versions had up-dos and frizz, and '90s releases often came with hair bands and miniature crimpers.

Buckaroo!

1970

The word Buckaroo is thought to come from the Spanish word 'vaquero', which refers to a man who takes care of cattle (although associations with the 'bucking' of a horse have also been made). The term is similar to 'cowboy' and is still used in rural areas of the United States.

Originally released by the Ideal Toy Company in 1970, the game featured a simple plastic mule and a number of items, such as a cowboy hat, a frying pan and a saddle.

Players must take turns to place these items on the back of this bad-tempered mule. If the player is careless, a spring will trigger and the mule will 'buck', kicking its hind legs upwards and dislodging all the items on its back. The winner is the player who manages to place all of the items on the mule's back without causing it to buck.

Over time, the game has been altered, and the mule is now more three-dimensional and wears a sardonic grin.

The German version of the game is named Cowboyschrek, which translates to 'cowboy fright'.

Mastermind is a code-breaking board game created in 1970 by Mordecai Meirowitz, an Israeli postmaster. Based on an earlier, pen-and-paper version called Bulls and Cows, the game involves two players, the codemaker and the codebreaker. The codemaker arranges a sequence of coloured pegs behind a screen. The codebreaker must place a row of pegs on the board in an attempt to guess the other player's pattern. Pins or tabs are used by the codemaker to signal whether the position or colour of the pegs is correct. The codebreaker has a limited number of turns to figure out the pattern, after which the players switch positions.

The box art for the original edition of the game has become iconic. Featuring a serious, suited man seated at a table, and a young female model standing behind him, the image portrayed a Bond-like supervillain and cast the player in the role of the hero.

In 1970, mathematician Donald Knuth calculated that it was possible to solve the code in five or fewer moves using a particular algorithm.

Mastermind

1970

Evel Knievel Stunt Cycle

1973

Robert Craig Knievel, known as Evel Knievel, was an American stunt performer popular in the sixties and seventies. Knievel was a phenomenon, performing stunt jumps over cars, buses, canyons and wild animals in the course of his career. As part of his promotion campaign, Knievel sold the rights to merchandise based on his name to the Ideal Toy Company, who began producing figures, outfits and accessories in 1972.

The Stunt Cycle was released in 1973, and became one of the most popular toys of the decade. The set consisted of a figurine of Knievel, wearing his trademark white suit, a motorbike and a red wind-up launcher. The bike and rider were placed on the launcher, and the wheel was turned, creating a loud revving noise. By pressing a button, the user could release the bike and send it speeding across the room, up a ramp, or over a line of toy cars.

Evel Knievel suffered 433 broken bones throughout his career, earning him a Guinness World Record for most broken bones in a lifetime.

Monchhichi

1974

On paper, a stuffed monkey with a plastic human face may not be the most commercial concept for a toy, but Monchhichi are an international phenomenon. They originated in Japan in 1974, with the stated aim of inspiring respect and love in the young and old, and were then launched in Western Europe and the USA in 1975 and 1980 respectively (licensed in the latter by Mattel until 1985). The range began with a boy and girl, but it has grown to include Monchhichi of various sizes, a Mother Care Monchhichi with a baby, grandparents, and countless outfits and accessories. After more than forty years, three television series and 70 million units sold, Koichi Sekiguchi, grandson of the company's founder, says that, 'Monchhichi is still delivering the same message of peace and love and will always be here to share his owner's joys and sorrows.'

In 1980, Monchhichi stopped sucking his thumb and was given a pacifier, after experts expressed concerns about children copying the toy, and developing orthodontic problems.

Playmobil

1974

The smiling face of the 'klicky', as the Playmobil figure is officially known, is a true icon of design. Its height, at just under three inches, was chosen in relation to the size of a child's hands, and its simple, happy face reflects the way that children draw people. All have the same expression, creating a blank canvas for role play, and the Playmobil universe is vast, offering endless sources of inspiration. The first sets were themed around Native Americans, knights and construction workers, but now everything from the Antarctic to the Zoo is represented, with 250 toys currently in production. More than 2.9 billion figures have been manufactured since 1974; according to Playmobil, if these figures held hands, they would circle the Earth 3.6 times.

Every second, the world's population increases by 2.6 people, but the population of the Playmobil world increases by 3.2 klickies.

Stretch Armstrong

1976

The first Stretch Armstrong, a blond muscle-man in pair of tiny black trunks, was a very innovative type of action figure. His latex-rubber skin was filled with corn syrup, which meant that when stretched he grew up to five feet tall, before slowly shrinking back to his original fifteen inches. He was a huge hit for Christmas 1976 and endured a lot of extremely spirited physical play, meaning that good-condition originals are extremely rare and valuable today. Due to popular demand, Stretch Armstrong was relaunched by Cap Toys in 1993, with a new look to match the style of the early 1990s. Disney bought the film rights to the toy in 1994, and various interpretations have been floated in the intervening two decades, but it would appear that the challenge of building a plot of a big budget, two-hour film around the character is simply too much of a stretch.

More than sixty international versions of Stretch Armstrong have been sold around the globe, including Mister Muscolo in Italy, Mr X in Japan, and El Hombre Elastico in Mexico.

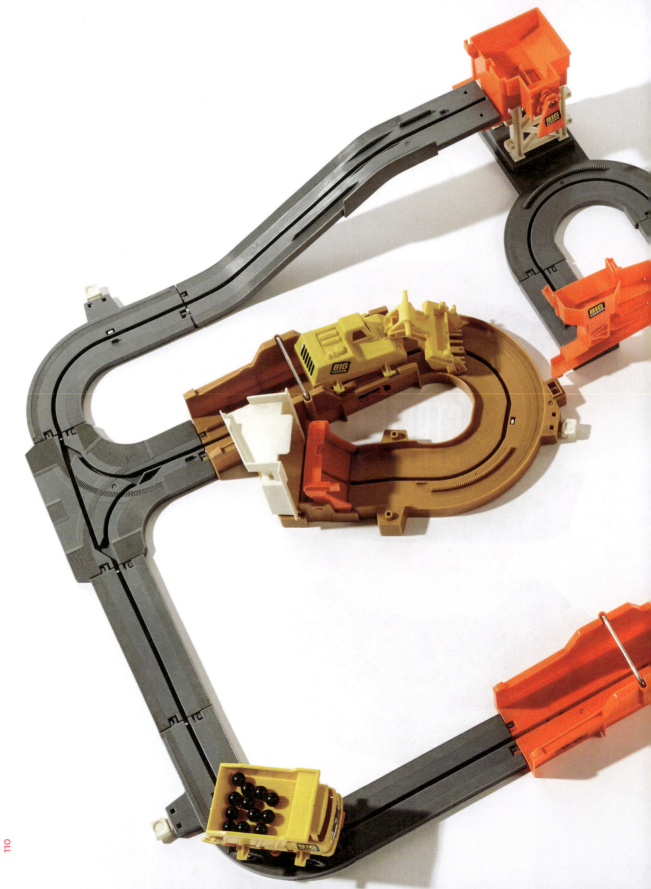

Big Loader
Construction Set

1977

The unassuming Big Loader, with its dump truck, ramp, delivery chute and scoop lifter, has won legions of dedicated fans since it hit the market. The industrious truck trundles around the eight feet of track, with its cargo of spherical plastic 'rocks', in an almost hypnotic fashion, and this looping nature makes it a valuable learning tool, helping in the development of sequential thinking. A Thomas the Tank Engine version has been extremely successful, and the Big Loader is very big in Japan, where budding builders could buy a Disney *Cars* Big Loader and even a pink Big Loader set (pleasingly, no changes were made to the toy other than the colour and some cheerful eyes on the vehicles). Pitched for children between three and seven, the Big Loader has the power to gently captivate boys and girls of all ages.

'The Construction Set that does it all. Loads, fills, scoops, switches, hauls, dumps and reverses. Truckin' around construction town, Big Loader picks 'em up and lays 'em down.'

Star Wars

1977

Star Wars is one of the most influential and popular science-fiction franchises of all time. The first instalment of George Lucas's epic space opera was released in 1977, and the franchise that evolved from the saga holds the Guinness World Record for 'most successful film merchandising franchise'. Few things have affected pop culture as dramatically as *Star Wars*. The franchise has such a large place in popular culture that in 2014 a documentary entitled *Plastic Galaxy: The Story of Star Wars Toys* was released. Among the myriad of toys produced was the All Terrain Armoured Transport, known as the AT-AT, an assault machine of the Galactic Empire. The military robot was based on the Paraceratherium, an extinct genus of rhino that was once one of the largest terrestrial mammals on the planet. Now a collector's item, the AT-AT toy is worth over $500.

Several newly discovered organisms have been named after characters from the *Star Wars* franchise, such as Han Solo, a species of trilobite, and Darthvaderum, an orbited mite.

Cabbage Patch Kids

1978

Created by Xavier Roberts, the Cabbage Patch Kids range was accorded the status of one of the most influential toys of all times by *Time* magazine, and is considered one of the most recognised brands in the world. More than 130 million Cabbage Patch Kids and their hand-made predecessors, the Little People, have been welcomed and loved as family members around the globe since 1978.

The Cabbage Patch Kids global phenomenon struck in 1983 when toy manufacturer Coleco introduced these unique dolls, with their own individual name, birth certificate and adoption papers. The brand generated more than $6 billion in revenue in just over thirty-five years. From the cover of *Time* magazine to becoming the official mascot of the US Olympic Team, the Cabbage Patch Kids have earned a place in society not often reserved for a toy brand.

BabyLand General Hospital, home of the Cabbage Patch Kids, gives this global family southern roots in the mountain community of Cleveland, Georgia.

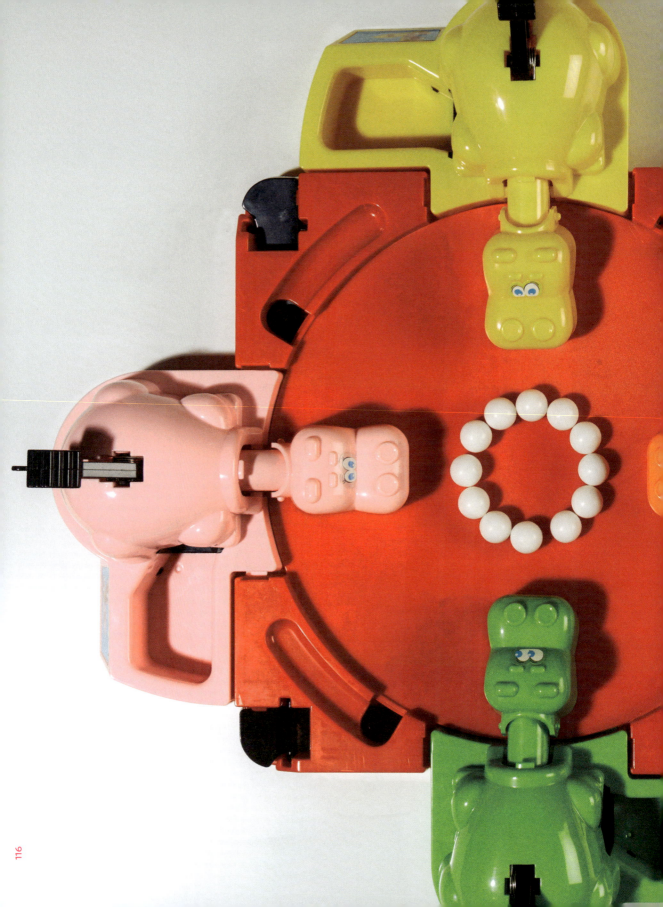

Hungry Hungry Hippos

1978

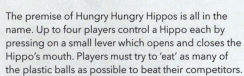

The premise of Hungry Hungry Hippos is all in the name. Up to four players control a Hippo each by pressing on a small lever which opens and closes the Hippo's mouth. Players must try to 'eat' as many of the plastic balls as possible to beat their competitors.

Created in 1967 by Fred Kroll, the game wasn't released until 1978, in the midst of the board-game craze that swept the seventies. The game is fast, frantic and noisy, which goes a long way towards explaining its popularity among generations of children.

Enterprising fans around the world have discovered a way to re-enact Hungry Hungry Hippos in real life by using a roller, a bucket and a lot of balls. The participants work in groups of two: one lies flat on a roller while the other stands and pulls their partner's legs inwards and outwards. The player lying on the ground must use a bucket to capture more balls than their opponent to win.

Each hippo is individually named: Henry Hippo (orange), Homer Hippo (green), Harry Hippo (yellow) and Lizzie Hippo (pink).

Cozy Coupe

1979

The Cozy Coupe was designed for Ohio-based toy manufacturer Little Tikes, and first released onto the market in 1979. With a high yellow dome and a bright red body, the Cozy Coupe was designed to mimic a real car, complete with a steering wheel and opening doors. The plastic moulding created a durable and light design, and the open floor allowed a child to propel themselves along by using their feet.

The car proved popular with both children and parents, and by 1991, over 500,000 units were being sold per year in the United States. A redesign was undertaken in 1999 which added thicker support pillars and a sturdier structure. For the thirtieth anniversary, the design was updated again to include removable floorboards, a handle on the back, a cup holder and a large, smiling face. In 2009, Rakesh Patel, owner of the first Cozy Coupe ever made, donated the car to the Crawford Auto-Aviation Museum in Cleveland.

In 1991, the Cozy Coupe was named the best-selling car in America, beating out competitors such as Ford, Honda and Toyota.

Guess Who?

1979

Theo and Ora Coster, who later became known as Theora Design, created the concept for Guess Who? in 1979, and the toy was first produced by Milton Bradley. The object of the game is to guess which character card the other player has selected from the pile. Players narrow down the selection by asking yes or no questions about hair and eye colour, whether the character is wearing a hat or glasses, and so on. As the questions are answered, players flip down the relevant characters on the board and, using a process of elimination, are left with the correct answer.

The composition of the characters has been the source of some controversy, with some customers complaining about a lack of racial and gender diversity. Original versions contained predominately white male characters, but over the years, new faces have been included and Hasbro now offers personalised character sheets depending on the players' country.

Theo Coster, designer of Guess Who?, was born in Amsterdam in 1928. Coster was a schoolmate of Anne Frank, and would walk with her to school before their families went into hiding from the Gestapo.

Rubik's Cube

1980

Hungarian sculptor and professor of architecture Erno Rubik came up with a prototype 'Magic Cube' in 1974 to demonstrate spatial relationships to his students. Their enthusiasm led him to look into manufacturing options, but Hungary's place behind the Iron Curtain meant that exports were tightly controlled.

In 1979, a Hungarian expat agreed to take Rubik's invention to the Nuremberg Toy Fair, where it caught the attention of toy specialist Tom Kremer. Kremer's faith in the cube led to the Ideal Toy Company deciding to distribute it internationally, and a 1980s icon was born. Worried that the name invoked connotations of witchcraft, the company decided on Rubik's Cube, after its inventor.

With 43 quintillion possible combinations, the Rubik's Cube is a challenging puzzle that can take hours or days to solve. Measuring 3 × 3 × 3 inches, the cube is made up of individual sides that move on an internal pivot.

Despite the notorious difficulty of the puzzle, 'speedcubers' have made a sport out of solving the Rubik's Cube as fast as possible, and as of 2015 the record stands at 4.9 seconds.

Fashion Wheel

1980

The Fashion Wheel was a treasured toy of budding young Vivienne Westwoods and Donna Karans everywhere. The sections of the wheel rotated, allowing you to line up the perfect hairstyle, top or jacket, and then skirt or trousers, with intervening sections for added patterns and textures. An impression was then made with the black wax crayon, before adding colour. Six options for each element created thousands of combinations, so this relatively simple and portable toy offered hours of stimulating and creative play. Over the years, the wheel itself has taken on a more luminous colour scheme, but happily the designs themselves have not changed much; it has kept its nostalgic feel and in fact, as fashion inevitably comes full circle, the Fashion Wheel's offerings could pass as the perfect modern hipster capsule wardrobe.

Later versions of the Fashion Wheel have included scenery to allow young designers to stage their own fashion shows.

Mr Frosty

1980

Released under the Playskool division of Hasbro in the 1980s, Mr Frosty was a toy that allowed children to create ice pops, slushies and fruit-flavoured drinks at home. Ice cubes were placed in the snowman's head and a handle was turned to produce crushed ice. Syrup sachets were included, which were mixed with water and sugar to create flavouring. Mr Frosty has been redesigned numerous times, with changes made to the mechanism and accessories, but the toy still retains the original snowman shape. The brand was licensed to Flair Leisure Products in 2015.

The original flavourings came in luminous packets and included Loopy Lemon, Outrageous Orange and Cheery Cherry.

Big Yellow Teapot

1981

Torquil Norman has led the kind of colourful life expected of the archetypal inventor: a former British fighter pilot and Wall Street Banker, and current arts philanthropist, he established Bluebird Toys in 1980, and the following year he released the Big Yellow Teapot. In combining two toy favourites – the doll's house and the tea set – Norman created a must-have for toddlers of the 1980s. Its simplified form, smooth surfaces and chunky pieces were perfect for little hands, and it became one of the most popular toys of the decade.

The Big Yellow Teapot came with a cheerful family of four and their dog, who could relax in the comfort of their now delightfully retro interiors, go for a drive in the teacup car, or enjoy a whirl on the roundabout concealed under the teapot's lid. In throwing out the rulebook for traditional doll-house design, the Big Yellow Teapot sparked a number of competing doll's houses, and the 'container' format remains a staple of the toy shop to this day.

The family dog in the Big Yellow Teapot is called Sugarlump.

Glo-Worm

1982

First released in 1982, the Glo-Worm functioned both
as a nightlight and a soft cuddly toy. With a long green
body and a smiling face, the pyjama-clad toy would light
up when squeezed, making it ideal for young children to
take to bed. Story books, games and other merchandise
soon became part of the Glo-Worm franchise. In 1986,
a range of plastic toys called Glo Friends were released,
and a short-lived TV show segment soon followed.

In 2005, the toy was changed due to safety concerns
regarding the materials used in its production. Later
designs were geared towards younger children, and the
most recent version of the Glo-Worm can sing a number
of lullabies as well as lighting up when pressed.

**In the 1986 television adaptation of
the Glo Friends line, Baby Glo-Worm is
voiced by Nancy Cartwright, who also
provides the voice for Bart Simpson.**

Super Soaker

1982

Lonnie Johnson, an engineer and part-time inventor, first came up with the idea for the Super Soaker while working for the US Airforce in 1982. The toy works by manually pressurising water using a pump, so that it shoots out of the nozzle at a high speed in a concentrated stream.

Originally named the Power Drencher, Johnson's invention was picked up by Larami Toys, who rebranded it as the Super Soaker in 1991 and launched it alongside a successful advertising campaign. During the 1990s, a number of incidents where real guns were drawn during water fights led to a call for a ban on Super Soakers, but Larami suggested that politicians should focus on gun control instead of water-gun control, and the issue was dropped. Super Soakers went on to become an iconic toy of the 1990s. Hasbro acquired the Larami brand in 2002, and in 2015, the Super Soaker was nominated for the US National Toy Hall of Fame.

'If you come to Neverland, it's a rule that you are bound to get wet.' During the 1990s, singer Michael Jackson and child actor Macaulay Culkin famously had large-scale water fights with Super Soakers on Jackson's Neverland Ranch.

AIR PRESSURE SUPER SOAKER 50

★ 1st Performance Pump Rapidly Between Shots

LARAMI

Care Bears

1982

Care Bears first appeared on a range of greeting cards for American Greetings in 1981, hand-drawn by illustrator Elena Kucharik. One year later, Kenner, in tandem with American Greetings, began producing a line of ten plush toys – Bedtime Bear, Birthday Bear, Cheer Bear, Friend Bear, Funshine Bear, Good Luck Bear, Grumpy Bear, Love-a-lot Bear, Tenderheart Bear and Wish Bear – each a different colour and identifiable by the 'Belly Badge' symbol on their stomachs.

The Care Bears' Hollywood career kicked off around the same time, with TV specials such as *The Care Bears in the Land Without Feelings* airing in 1983. A feature film followed in 1985, and spin-offs and sequels continued to appear throughout the 1980s. The success of the Care Bears on screen, and the addition of a wider range of characters, led to over 40 million plush bears being sold between 1983 and 1987.

With a brief lull in the 1990s, Care Bears was relaunched in 2002, with over 90 million plush bears sold between 2002 and 2007. Relaunched yet again in 2015 with toy partner Just Play, and a brand new Netflix Original series, Care Bears and their wholesome message of caring and sharing continue to resonate with audiences. Care Bears will celebrate their thirty-fifth anniversary in 2017.

The Care Bears regularly faced off against enemies such as No Heart and his henchman Beastly by using a ray of light from their stomachs, initiated with the chant, 'Care Bears Count Down!'

Jenga

1983

During the 1970s, while living in Ghana, Leslie Scott's family would play with wooden blocks from a local sawmill. Scott's friends liked the game so much that she eventually decided to put it on the market. Having grown up speaking Swahili, Scott decided to give the game the name of 'Jenga', which means 'build'. Jenga was first launched at the 1983 London Toy Fair, but sales were slow. It wasn't until the 1986 Toronto Toy Fair that the game really took off.

Jenga is played by first stacking the wooden blocks in a tower. Each player then takes a turn at carefully removing a block, and placing it on the top. As the game progresses, the tower becomes more unstable and the game becomes more difficult. The person who causes the tower to fall over is the loser.

Various versions have been released, including Jenga Xtreme, which uses blocks shaped as parallelograms rather than the traditional rectangular shape. A giant version has also been released that can reach heights of eight feet.

Robert Grebler is said to hold the record for the highest Jenga tower ever built, at 40⅔ levels.

137

My Little Pony

1983

In 1981, Hasbro released a precursor to the My Little Pony range – a large plastic horse figurine named My Pretty Pony and designed by Bonnie Zacherle. This original toy was popular, and so in 1983 Hasbro decided to redesign the model, reduce the size and rename the series. With long, brushable hair, plastic bodies and child-friendly names such as Cotton Candy and Butterscotch, the first Ponies were an immediate success. The series expanded to include Unicorn Ponies, Sea Ponies and Pegasus Ponies, each with their own special attributes. My Little Pony releases have since been categorised by collectors into 'generations', with each featuring rare or unusual Ponies that are always in high demand.

The Ponies made their first television appearance in 1984, and a movie followed in 1986, featuring the voices of such illustrious figures as Danny DeVito and Tony Randall. After a number of reboots, the series underwent a successful revival in 2010 to coincide with the release of the television series *My Little Pony: Friendship is Magic*. The popularity of this show outside of its intended target audience came as a surprise to Hasbro, with a large and varied adult fandom exploding internationally and online. The series continues to grow and expand, and a feature-length movie is planned for 2017.

Older, male fans of My Little Pony are known as 'bronies', a combination of the words 'bro' and 'pony'.

Pound Puppies

1984

Pound Puppies was a plush toy line invented by
Mike Bowling in 1984, and introduced to the
American market by Tonka. Taking the shape of a
soft, cuddly dog with drooping eyelids and floppy
ears, each Pound Puppy was 'adopted' by its new
owner. Every dog came in a cardboard dog house,
and accessories and other merchandise were also
available. Feline counterparts, known as Pound Pur-r-
ries, were released later, with a similar premise.

In 1985, veteran animation company Hanna-
Barbera released a television special based on the
franchise, followed by a two-season series in 1986.
The Pound Puppy craze died down in the nineties,
but the brand, now in the hands of Hasbro, was
revived in 2010 with a new series and toy line.

In 2012, an episode of the *Pound
Puppies* television series, 'I Never
Barked for My Father', received
the Humanitas Prize for film and
television writing promoting human
dignity, meaning and freedom.

Transformers

1984

In the 1980s, a number of transforming toys were on the market in Japan, and Hasbro, seeing this success, partnered with Takara Toys to condense these toys into one line – Transformers. The toys were humanoid figures that could change into vehicles, machines and animals. Each toy came with technical specifications and a character biography, along with a set of stickers.

The success of the franchise lay not only in the uniqueness of the toys, but in the depth and scope of the backstory. With histories that fleshed out each robot into an individual character, and the backdrop of a vast narrative universe, kids were hooked on the battle between the Autobots and the Decepticons. Led by Optimus Prime and Megatron, the two sides clashed in a battle of good versus evil that has extended through a number of generations, animated shows, comic books, video games and live-action films. Illustrating their enduring appeal, in 2007, a collection of 275 pieces of original Transformers merchandise, unboxed and in mint condition, was sold on eBay for $1 million.

'Transformers, robots in disguise, Transformers, more than meets the eye', went the original 1980s jingle, and some variation on these lyrics has been used to promote the brand ever since.

Keypers

1985

Keypers were a range of colourful animal toys with hard plastic bodies and benevolent smiling faces that masked a thrilling secret: each came with a large key that unlocked its torso, allowing their owner to hide all their most treasured possessions away from prying eyes and sticky fingers. The first Keypers included Fancy the Snail, Tango the Ladybird and Shelldon the Tortoise, and each was accompanied by a hairbrush and a little bespectacled friend called a Finder.

A second series was introduced in 1987, with animals taking more cartoon-like forms, and the third series, launched in 1990, included special musical and jewellery Keypers, but were visually another step away from the originals. As part pretty doll, part treasure chest, Keypers found a devoted fan base, and the range was expanded to include books, cartoons, puzzles, lunchboxes, soft furnishings and cuddly Keypers.

Alongside snails, ladybirds and tortoises, the Keypers menagerie included cats, dogs, rabbits, ponies, squirrels, swans, bears, penguins and kangaroos.

Teddy Ruxpin

1985

Ken Forsse worked for Disney's theme park division in
the 1960s and '70s, including on the famous animatronic
attraction 'It's a Small World', and he was inspired to create
a toy with these mechanical attributes that children could
own. Story-reading Teddy Ruxpin was born, complete with
a complex origin story and world called Grundo, but toy
companies were initially resistant. When Fosse and his
partners at Alchemy II tweaked the design to include a
two-track cassette that would synchronise the audio with
Teddy's movements, Worlds of Wonder decided to take
a chance and put it into production. Sales reached $93
million in its first year. A cartoon debuted in 1987, running
for sixty-five episodes, and Teddy Ruxpin was so beloved
that he was partnered with a number of awareness causes,
including the USA's National Centre for Missing and
Exploited Children.

**Phil Baron, who voiced Teddy Ruxpin
both in toy and cartoon form, was also
the voice of Piglet on Disney's *Welcome
to Pooh Corner*.**

Teenage Mutant Ninja Turtles

1988

The Teenage Mutant Ninja Turtles first appeared in a doodle by Kevin Eastman and Peter Laird in 1983. Taken with the idea, they set up a company and printed three thousand copies of an original comic book based on the characters. In 1987, Playmate Toys expressed an interest in producing a line of accompanying toys, but were keen on an animated cartoon to test the waters. An agreement was reached, and the TV series first aired in October 1988. With a memorable theme song, catchphrases such as 'heroes in a half shell' and 'turtle power', Donatello, Michelangelo, Leonardo and Raphael were a hit.

Playmate Toys released their first line of action figures in 1988 to coincide with the TV show. The first generation of figurines featured the four turtles and their signature weapons, along with characters such as April, Shredder and Splinter. The toys, along with the animated show, became a phenomenon, and for a decade, Turtlemania reigned. Director Michael Bay recently rebooted the franchise for the big screen, and Playmate Toys continue to release TMNT-themed merchandise.

In the UK, due to strict anti-violence censorship laws, the franchise was renamed as Teenage Mutant Hero Turtles, and Michelangelo even lost the use of his nunchucks.

Game Boy

1989

Gunpei Yokoi came up with the idea for a handheld game console after watching a train passenger fiddling with the buttons on a calculator. His first attempt, the Game & Watch, was released in 1980, and so began the rise of the portable entertainment system. Yokoi, who worked on many iconic Nintendo titles such as *Super Mario Bros.* and *Donkey Kong*, developed this idea further, resulting in the release of the Game Boy in 1989.

Launching with *Super Mario Bros.* in Japan, and a year later with *Tetris* in the US, the Game Boy was an instant success. Although the 8-bit graphics and monochrome screen may seem basic to modern eyes, the console was revolutionary, as were the quantity and calibre of game cartridges available for it.

The original console was followed by the Game Boy Color, the Game Boy Advance and the Nintendo DS, all of which built upon the strong legacy of the Nintendo name. Inducted into the US National Toy Hall of Fame in 2009, the design of the Game Boy is still iconic, and it makes frequent appearances in pop culture.

The Game Boy was the first gaming console to appeal equally to both genders, with female players making up 45 per cent of the market. This gap has continued to shrink, and recent studies have indicated that female gamers are now in the majority.

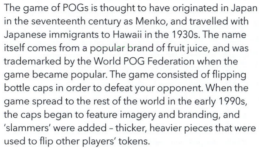

POGs

1990

The game of POGs is thought to have originated in Japan in the seventeenth century as Menko, and travelled with Japanese immigrants to Hawaii in the 1930s. The name itself comes from a popular brand of fruit juice, and was trademarked by the World POG Federation when the game became popular. The game consisted of flipping bottle caps in order to defeat your opponent. When the game spread to the rest of the world in the early 1990s, the caps began to feature imagery and branding, and 'slammers' were added – thicker, heavier pieces that were used to flip other players' tokens.

POGs were as collectible as they were playable, as the variations were endless. Every pop culture figure or franchise had their image emblazoned on a coin-sized piece of cardboard, along with logos, branding, celebrities and even politicians. POGs became such a craze that they were banned in many schools, as the practice of playing 'for keeps' was essentially a form of gambling. By the late 1990s, however, the fad had passed, and the brief reign of POGs gradually came to an end.

In 2001, during the Afghanistan war, the US military began to use POGs as a form of currency in order to cut down on the expense of shipping American coins to the Middle East.

Baby Born

1991

While some dolls have found success through wide ranges of accessories, realistic movements, or even speech, Baby Born took a different approach to attracting customers, with a focus on anatomical correctness and bodily functions. While other dolls with similar features had been on the market previously, Baby Born has demonstrated staying power, developing into a beloved worldwide brand.

Launched in 1991 by Zapf Creations, a German toy company founded in 1932, Baby Born favoured realism over fashion sense. Through an internal mechanism of tanks and tubes, the doll could eat, drink, cry and soil itself, allowing young children to play the role of devoted parent. Over the years, the doll has been developed and improved, with the latest version boasting eight lifelike functions. The accessory range has also expanded, to include bottles, bathtubs, potties, dummies, carriers and a whole wardrobe of outfits.

Many families use dolls such as Baby Born as potty-training aids. However, the doll's tendency to leak once upright may not send quite the right message.

Dream Phone

1991

'Oooh! Take a look at the gameboard! One of these twenty-four boys likes you! He was too shy to tell you himself, but he has told all of his friends. Now you have to call them for clues so you can find out WHO the Secret Admirer is!'

Dream Phone, a then-high-tech mystery game aimed at girls in their early teens, is the epitome of an early 1990s toy. With its Day-Glo colour palette and hot-pink cordless phone, it was a reimagining of 1960s game Mystery Date and was quickly established as a slumber-party essential. The object of the game is to be the first to discover which boy has a crush on everyone playing by 'calling' his friends for clues on the oversized dream phone and eliminating those who don't fit his ever-so dreamy profile.

Almost twenty-five years later, Dream Phone remains in the consciousness of nostalgic thirty-somethings, with *Cosmopolitan* publishing 'the definitive ranking of Dream Phone boyfriends'.

Talkboy

1992

Some debate surrounds the origins of the Talkboy, the hand-held voice recorder and burglar-evasion tool made famous by the 1992 Macaulay Culkin film *Home Alone 2: Lost in New York*. There is a popular theory that the Talkboy was merely a prop for the film that was hastily put into production in response to the film's popularity and the subsequent clamouring by young fans for the device. In fact, it was produced and ready for sale in the US on the day *Home Alone 2* was released. Several variations of the Talkboy followed, including the Deluxe model, which allowed for voice modulation, and the FX Plus, which took the form of a pen. The Talkgirl and Talkgirl Deluxe were also released; they were exactly the same, but pink…

According to E! the child actors who appeared in the *Home Alone 2* toy-store scene were each allowed to take home a toy; despite the fact that the model in the film didn't work, Macaulay Culkin chose the Talkboy.

Beanie Babies

1993

Ty Warner came up with the concept for an affordable and realistic plush toy in 1983 after a trip to Italy, and this idea would eventually evolve into the Beanie Babies phenomenon. Stuffed with small plastic pellets, or 'beans', the first nine toys were launched in 1993. Warner's strategy involved word-of-mouth marketing, limited production and a focus on smaller retail outlets instead of megastores. By the mid-1990s, Beanie Babies had become a craze, and children and collectors were clamouring to get their hands on as many as possible.

Each Beanie Baby came with a distinctive heart-shaped tag that featured the toy's name, birthdate and a poem. These became as important as the toy itself, with many retailers offering plastic containers specially designed to protect the tag. From ostriches to apes, snakes to dolphins, crabs to snails, the Beanie Babies range became vast and varied, with many collectors convinced that they would increase exponentially in value. While many did sell for large amounts online, the majority of toys never lived up to buyers' financial expectations.

In 2000, a royal-blue Peanut the Elephant Beanie Baby, one of the rarest ever made, was sold at an auction for $3,005.

Sky Dancers

1994

Sky Dancers were a line of toys popular with young girls during the 1990s. The toy was composed of a fairy-like figurine with foam wings which stood on a decorative plastic base. Using a pull-string mechanism, the doll would be launched into the air, causing the wings to spin like a propeller. The toy inspired a TV spin-off, which featured the flying fairies attending a dance academy. A version of the toy aimed at young boys, called Dragon Flyz, was released in 1996, along with another animated series.

Sky Dancers came with strict instructions to aim the toy away from any bystanders, but it was frequently the cause of injuries and was often weaponised by enterprising children. Due to this, Sky Dancers were pulled from the market in 2000. Jakks Pacific released a revamped version in 2005, but the appeal of an airborne toy has never again reached the dizzy heights of the 1990s.

The challenges of taming a Sky Dancer have been immortalised on the internet by a popular clip of a young girl who excitedly launches her fairy, only for it to drift gracefully across the room and into an open fireplace.

Buzz Lightyear

1995

The star of three blockbuster films, Buzz Lightyear needs little introduction. Lightyear rocketed to international fame with the release of *Toy Story* in 1995, and retailers couldn't keep up with the demand for the accompanying action figure. When the sequel was released, the manufacturers were better prepared and had added a new model with the utility belt worn by Lightyear in the film.

Lightyear was named after Buzz Aldrin, second man on the moon, and in 2008 Lightyear became the first toy astronaut in space; one of the original action figures flew on board the *Discovery* to the International Space Station, where he spent six months enjoying the views and the company of astronauts and cosmonauts. In 2012, this particular Buzz Lightyear retired to the National Air and Space Museum in Washington, D.C., but with *Toy Story 4* on the way, Buzz Lightyear's popularity looks certain to continue, 'to infinity … and beyond!'

The great Buzz Lightyear action figure drought of Christmas 1996 was due to the fact that Disney believed that Woody would be the runaway star of *Toy Story*. It is estimated that 50,000 Buzz Lightyears were made, compared to over 200,000 Woody action figures – a misstep that is said to have cost $300 million in lost sales.

Bop It

1996

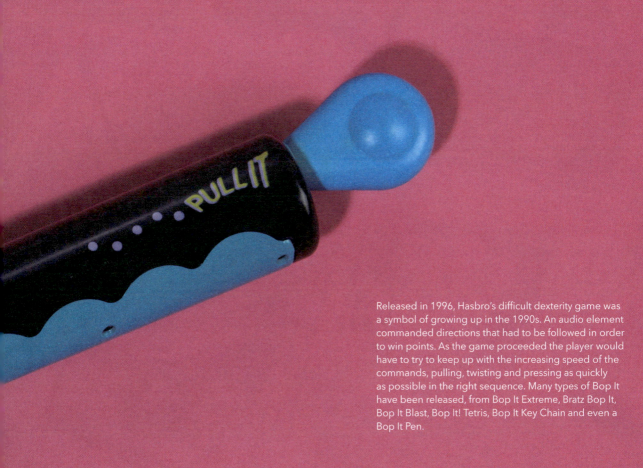

Released in 1996, Hasbro's difficult dexterity game was a symbol of growing up in the 1990s. An audio element commanded directions that had to be followed in order to win points. As the game proceeded the player would have to try to keep up with the increasing speed of the commands, pulling, twisting and pressing as quickly as possible in the right sequence. Many types of Bop It have been released, from Bop It Extreme, Bratz Bop It, Bop It Blast, Bop It! Tetris, Bop It Key Chain and even a Bop It Pen.

Bop It appears in the popular television show *Gilmore Girls*, where it is used to liven up an awkward social situation.

Pokémon Cards

1996

Pokémon was invented by Satoshi Tajiri in 1995. Inspired by his love of insect-collecting, a popular past-time in Japan, he created an intricate world of 'pocket monsters' that became a global sensation. It began as a video game that set trainers on a mission to capture and train wild Pokémon for battle – hence the catchphrase 'Gotta catch 'em all!' It was succeeded by a wildly popular anime series following a young trainer named Ash Ketchum. The collectible trading card game was invented in 1996 and retains a giant cult following of children and adults. Today the *Pokémon* franchise has an estimated worth of $24 billion.

July 2016 saw the release of Pokémon GO, an app that allows fans to capture and train virtual Pokémon in real time using a smartphone. The concept originated as an April Fool's joke, but the response was so great that the game was developed for real, and it has been credited with popularising augmented reality.

Tamagotchi

1996

A portmanteau of the Japanese word *tamago* (egg) and the English word 'watch', Tamagotchis first hit the global market in 1996, and quickly became a fad. A small, palm-sized computer, it was billed as 'the world's first virtual pet', and the futuristic toys seemed to provide all the fun of a pet without any of the mess. Users had to care for their on-screen pet by feeding, treating and disciplining it as it moved through a number of life cycles. The pet would beep for attention, driving a generation of parents and teachers crazy, but cleaning up digital droppings seemed to hold an endless appeal for children. If left for too long, the Tamagotchi would 'die', so the challenge lay in racking up as many virtual days as possible.

Modern incarnations of the Tamagotchi include features such as games and connectivity, allowing two players to link their toys. From a twenty-first-century perspective, these advancements seem tame when compared to more high-tech products, but for '90s kids, a Tamagotchi was the height of cool, especially when worn hanging from a belt loop.

When the virtual pets died, the Japanese version would display a ghost and a tombstone on the screen. For more sensitive European market, an angel was shown. Today, online cemeteries exist where users can mourn their digital friends.

Tickle Me Elmo

1996

Tickle Me Elmo, based on the popular children's character from *Sesame Street*, was a plush toy introduced by Tyco Toys in 1996. Ron Dubren, along with Greg Hyman, came up with a prototype for a toy that would laugh and vibrate when tickled, and presented it to Tyco in 1992. After a few false starts, the fuzzy red character of Elmo was decided upon for the design, and the familiar giggle made the toy a must-have for children everywhere.

However, when parents tried to match their children's enthusiasm, chaos descended. A plug on *The Rosie O'Donnell Show* in October 1996 sent demand into the stratosphere, and low supplies meant that the Christmas market became infected with 'Elmo-mania'. Arrests, assaults and stampedes all featured in the shopping frenzy that ensued, and the black-market value of Tickle Me Elmo soared to thousands of dollars. Demand has remained high ever since, and for the tenth anniversary of the toy, Mattel, which obtained the Tyco brand in 1997, released Elmo TMX (Tickle Me eXtreme). This rerelease was shrouded in secrecy and came in packaging that resembled a lock box.

In December 1996, at the height of Elmo-mania, a number of newspapers reported that a reputed crime boss in New York managed to procure a number of sold-out Tickle Me Elmos under suspicious circumstances.

Furby

1998

Marketed as an animatronic toy capable of interacting with humans, the Furby was officially launched at the 1998 American International Toy Fair by Tiger Electronics. With a furry, owl-like appearance, a Furby could blink, move and react to the user, creating an effect of apparent intelligence. The toys spoke an invented language called 'Furbish', and could learn and replace certain phrases with their English equivalents.

With 40 million units sold in the first three years of production, the Furby was a defining toy of the late nineties. Its immediate popularity meant that production could not keep up with international demand, and the resale value soared to multiples of the initial retail price.

The original Furby has been updated multiple times to add more expressions, emotions and movements. The latest incarnation comes with an app that allows the user to teach, play and interact with their Furby, firmly propelling the toy into the digital age.

In 1999, due to their ability to record and repeat information, Furbies were considered a security threat and were banned from the National Security Agency's premises in Maryland, USA.

Alien Eggs

1999

One of the odder trends of the 1990s, Alien Eggs became a playground must-have in 1999. Ostensibly from the planet Scardox, these aliens came curled up in a plastic shell surrounded by a coloured goo. Perhaps due to their bizarre premise, a number of urban legends sprung up surrounding these creatures: in some circles, the aliens were to open their eyes at the stroke of midnight on 31 December 1999; others were rumoured to give birth, after a complicated process that could involve anything from freezing the egg to placing it in the microwave. Later versions did come with the ability to 'birth' smaller versions from holes in their backs or head. Alien Eggs can still be found in shops today, but savvy children are more likely to fling these gooey oddities against a wall than suspect an extra-terrestrial awakening.

In November 1999, a discarded Alien Egg was found on a London underground platform and rushed to hospital, mistaken for a human foetus.

Beyblades

2000

Beyblades, first released by Takara Tomy in 2000, are a line of spinning tops that are used in 'battles' between two or more players. Made up of a plastic top and a rip-cord launcher, the toys are fired at high speed into a specially designed arena. The toys bounce off each other as they spin, and the last top remaining upright is the winner. Beyblades are based on an ancient Japanese spinning-top game called *beigoma*, which has a similar premise and remains popular in traditional areas of Japan.

The launch of the toy line coincided with the release of an anime series that focuses on a group of children who take part in Beyblade battles. Each Beyblade is different, and has different specialities such as attack, defence and stamina. Some maintain, however, that there is very little skill involved in the game, and that luck plays a greater role than any other factor. Beyblades became a fad in the 2000s, and it was reported that some parents were taking their children on 'Beydates' (Beyblade playdates).

'Three, two, one, let it rip!' is the battlecry that heralds the start of a Beyblade battle.

Bratz

2001

Yasmin, Cloe, Jade and Sasha hit the scene in a somewhat modest fashion in 2001, but by 2005 Bratz had amassed sales of $2 billion, and the range was established as a real competitor to Barbie, whose reign had been unchallenged for decades. They are perhaps the most divisive dolls in the toy shop, with their extreme proportions, heightened features, and edgy clothes and make-up, but their ethnic diversity and fashion-forward style was ahead of its time. The Bratz world expanded rapidly, to include numerous doll lines, films, games and apps, and in 2015 an overhaul of the brand was unveiled, including a new core doll, Raya. All Bratz dolls are designed by two fashion designers in LA, and the marketing is directed at a generation that hasn't known a world without Youtube and Instagram – indeed, one of the of the range's biggest recent success stories was the 'Selfie' doll.

The Bratz designers have a keen eye and fast hands when it comes to PR; their popular Instagram feed has featured Bratz versions of Taylor Swift, Caitlin Jenner, Vivienne Westwood and even Frida Kahlo.

Squinkies

2010

Miniature toys have been popular as collectables for centuries, and in 2010, Squinkies became the latest craze to hit the market. Squinkies are small, collectable figurines that come in plastic, egg-like containers called 'bubbles', similar to gumball dispensables that were popular in previous decades. Made of latex-free squishy and squashy plastic, their various figures include pets, human-like figures and exotic animals. Squinkies can be used as pencil toppers, and often come in playsets and with accessories. Some variations are rare, adding to their collectability, and others are only available at certain retailers. A number of commentators have linked the Squinkies phenomenon to the Great Recession of the late 2000s, arguing that the pocket-friendly prices made them an appealing option for parents.

According to *The Wall Street Journal*, the popularity of Squinkies is linked to the desire to collect, sort and categorise objects, which is part of a child's natural cognitive development.

Minecraft

2011

Today, it is rare for a toy to be launched without a whole cast of characters, and preferably a TV show and a feature-length movie. If the toy is successful, it is not uncommon for a video game to appear. In the case of *Minecraft*, this process occurred in reverse. First released in 2011, *Minecraft* is a simple block placement sandbox game that encourages resource gathering, crafting and combat. *Minecraft* became immensely popular with younger gamers due to the simple and self-directed gameplay, creative opportunities and multiplayer mode. The game is procedurally generated, leading to a virtually infinite landscape, and the player gathers resources to build vast, blocky structures and defeat enemy characters. From this success has spawned an entire range of clothes, collectables, competitions and toys, including actions figures and pixelated foam weapons. While not a toy in the traditional sense, the incredible success of *Minecraft* demonstrates how the toy market – and the very definition of a toy – is always changing.

In 2014, the Danish government used *Minecraft* to recreate their entire nation in an attempt to pique children's interest in geography. Unfortunately, the digital nation was attacked by 'America', causing an in-game diplomatic incident.

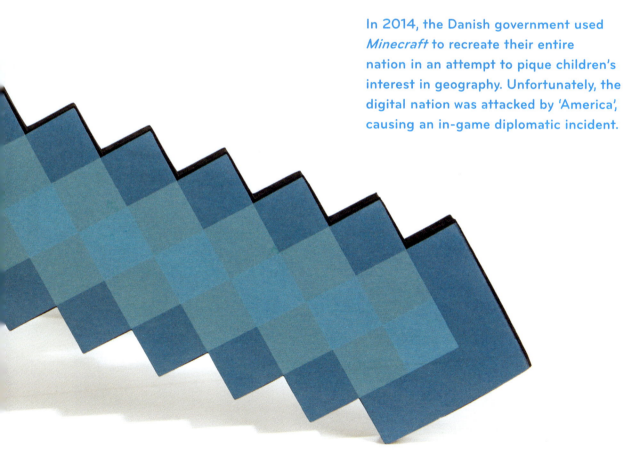

Rainbow Loom

2011

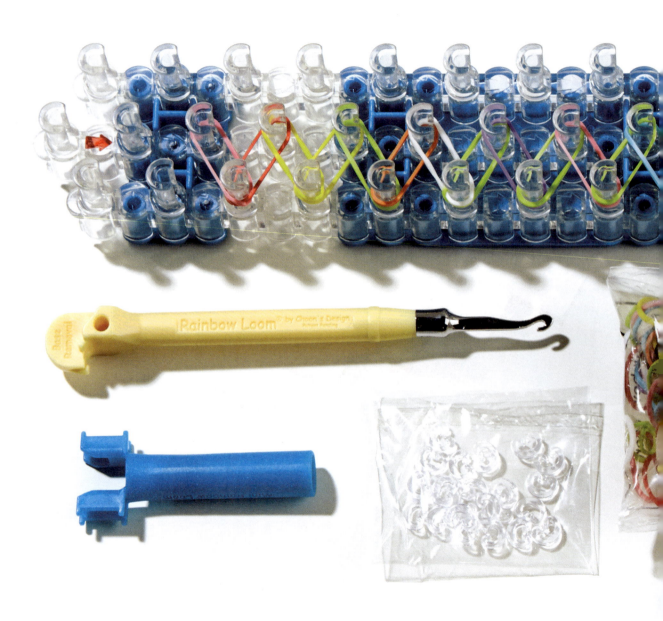

Rainbow Loom is a weaving tool used for creating bracelets and jewellery from rubber bands. Created by engineer Cheong Choon Ng in 2011 as a way to impress his two teenage daughters, the loom is made up of a plastic board with a number of pegs which can be used to loop rubber bands together. The knots, known as Brunnian links, can then be made into colourful jewellery. The technique employed is similar to one used to make rubber jump ropes in Ng's native Malaysia, and when local children expressed interest in his daughters' bracelets, Ng decided to invest in his product. American retailers did not show enthusiasm initially, but Ng created a number of online tutorials and the craze took off. Children everywhere became expert weavers, creating and swapping the bracelets in playgrounds around the world.

Celebrities such as Kate Middleton, Miley Cyrus, Harry Styles, David Beckham and even Pope Francis have all been spotted wearing loom bands.

Lottie

2012

Lottie, the brainchild of Ian Harkin and Lucie Follet, came about as a response to other fashion dolls on the toy market, many of whom, it has been claimed, are unrealistic, overly sexualised, and would even have to walk on all fours if they were real, due to their distorted proportions.

The company Arklu began in 2001 by creating a line of dolls inspired by Princess Kate Middleton, and from this experience they decided that there was an appetite for a wholesome alternative to current offerings.

The doll is based on the anatomical proportions of a nine-year-old child, does not come with makeup or jewellery, and her clothing is in line with that of a real child. The models are ethnically diverse, age-appropriate, and can stand unaided – a simple task that many other dolls on the market have failed to master. Lottie's activities are gender neutral, and the company places an emphasis on body positivity, outdoor activity and educational pursuits.

In 2015, in collaboration with the European Space Agency, the company released Stargazer Lottie, which became the first doll to go into space.

Kinetic Sand

2013

Kinetic Sand is mixture of 98 per cent sand and 2 per cent polydimethylsiloxane, which is a silicon oil also used in Silly Putty that makes the sand stick to itself but not to other surfaces. The result is a material with the tactile sensation of wet sand without the mess, making it perfect for indoor play. Kinetic Sand is a thoroughly modern addition to the toy box – non-toxic and gluten-free, it allows apartment dwellers to bring the outdoors inside to enjoy hours of calming and creative play. It is also widely used in occupational therapy with children, helping to develop motor skills and sensory processing, and in increasing attention span. The therapeutic benefits of playing with Kinetic Sand are not limited to children, however, with hordes of adults finding themselves hypnotised by the substance. The manufacturers say that it 'breathes motion', and indeed it can seem to have a life of its own. It is easy to shape and mould, before slowly melting in front of your eyes.

The US Department of Defense uses Kinetic Sand to study and prepare for natural disasters; its malleable and shape-shifting qualities make it the perfect material to sculpt what they refer to as a 'tangible landscape'.

Frozen Dolls

2013

Inspired by Hans Christian Andersen's 'The Snow Queen', *Frozen* is the heart-warming story of aristocratic sisters Anna and Elsa. Released in 2013 by Disney, the CGI animation has become a billion-dollar franchise and is the highest-grossing animated film ever. The film has an ardent and loyal fandom and the demand for merchandise is gigantic. Christmas 2014 saw an international meltdown, as parents scrambled to purchase Anna and Elsa dolls for their demanding children. A toy retailer was quoted as saying, 'We could sell empty boxes with Frozen written on them at the moment.'

Limited edition Elsa and Anna dolls have sold on eBay for as much as $10,000.

THE
ART OF
THE TOY

Stevanne Auerbach,
PhD/Dr. Toy™

THE HISTORY
OF TOYS

There is a great deal to learn about the past from the history of toys. Going back to ancient civilisations, toys show up in the earliest archives. Children played with bone, clay, reeds, stones, sticks, and pieces of fabric, feathers, fur, and other found objects.

For a long time, toys strongly reflected the life of the times, as you can see from the types of toys used one hundred years ago. Today, there are toys that reflect current civilisation, complete with technology embedded in video games, cell phones, computers, and video art products. Years ago, before multimedia, computers, and handheld devices, our entertainment was simple, direct and easy. We played with natural objects around us, both inside and outside of our homes and schools. We played with basic toys we often created ourselves, or our grandfather made with his own hands. We can easily recall happy memories of playing with basic toys like crayons, finger paint, Play-Doh, or amazing fun toys made out of metal, plastic or wood (great toys, yes, but today they might not pass stricter toy safety tests).

In the years ahead we may be ready for a renaissance of new products based again on the old. The toy marketplace is dynamic, transitory, and stimulating. But we always need to be clear about the objectives of the toy and what the intentions are for play. Ultimately, with each new product, we need to ask ourselves, 'Is this a toy that deserves a lasting place in the child's toy chest?'

WHAT MAKES
A GOOD TOY?

A good toy should not require magic, parental assembly, elaborate instructions, or an advanced degree to make it work. Rather, a good toy is ready to be discovered as soon as it comes out of its attractive, colourful and informative box. It should be designed well and be durable; it should reflect the best in design, be fun and safe, and provide optimal benefits for children. The child should be able to easily discover the toy's play value.

For parents, it is sometimes a challenge to locate appropriate toys in the wide world of playthings. Great toys often do not even need TV advertising, since their value spreads by word of mouth, and on parenting blogs. Sometimes advertising can actually be detrimental and distracting, and can give exaggerated impressions of the product's merits only to fail to deliver in real-life play situations.

Many toys fail to hold a child's interest in repeat play soon after the child takes it out of the box, but the best toys remain popular over generations because they are durable, have a wide variety of attributes, are educational, practical, and, of course, deliver fun – the most basic ingredient. Some long-lasting, widely enjoyed and well-designed products include building blocks, crayons, dolls, puzzles, hula hoops, jump ropes, stacking rings, trains, yo-yos and teddy bears.

Toys offer social opportunity, and a chance for the child to have fun, learn and grow, both alone and in company, with good toys encouraging children to interact, socialise, and communicate with one another. Great toys promote affection, communication, creativity, help to constructively influence social and gender roles, and provide activities to effectively utilise children's time. This book celebrates many enduring classic playthings that meet the identified criteria, have survived over time, and continue to stimulate each coming generation. We can look back to the magic of the past, as we move with greater insight and wisdom into the future, and simultaneously foster the creativity of tomorrow.

TOYS & LEARNING

We know that children in early years learn best through play: they gain co-ordination and brain development. And so they need the stimulation that a variety of playthings provide to ensure they reach their full potential. When children discover objects like the Furby, Slinky or Tonka Truck, they learn to expand skills of placing and pushing objects, exploration, discovery, and the joy of surprise.

Good toys have multiple purposes and are adaptable, so as the child gains control, the fun and learning increases. Many offer developmental skill-building, such as matching, sorting, colours, and shapes, as illustrated by Meccano, Playmobil and the Rubik's Cube.

Alongside developing a wide variety of skills, toys should help children gain appreciation of aesthetics. For example, in developing personal creativity and manual dexterity, construction toys are a perfect stimulant. With the right construction product at their fingertips, children become connected to their own creativity, finding many different ways to build, make their own creations, be inventive, and use their imagination. Learning to build and tear apart is the focus of Lego and other blocks, which are among the best open-ended, multifaceted of toys. The child's brain, imagination and physical dexterity are stimulated, and it is a wonderful way to discover the expanding excitement of building. Variations to the basics keep busy little builders moving their hands with a hammer, screwdriver and wrench.

To enhance mental processes, board games are perfect. Children can also play with well-designed technology that allows them to use animation and to display and obtain information while gaining confidence and expanding many important skills.

Active toys include a great variety of outdoor, construction and adventure play. This form of play helps children develop co-ordination and manipulation skills. Children also enjoy 'destructive' play, actively taking things apart

and tearing them down. Active play helps to improve children's physical ability, and to develop their abilities in climbing, crawling and jumping.

Educational play involves language, science, math, hobbies and special interests, which include games, puzzles and projects. Perfect complements for these activities are versatile products that allow the child to engage in and move between activities.

WHAT MAKES A TOY AN ART FORM?

Toys are the first 'art experience' of childhood. When children play with toys, they learn to appreciate form, shape and colour, just as adults appreciate the same qualities when they view a painting or sculpture. The artful toy provides enjoyment, lasting play value, and has proven to be well worth the price. It continues to sell as it is a staple in the marketplace. Let us look closely for a moment at the art of the toy as illustrated by well-designed products included in this eclectic book: the classic play of art and discovery are seamlessly combined in Mr. Potato Head, Play-Doh, Silly Putty and the Rainbow Loom; eye-hand co-ordination is married to additional lessons in shapes while playing with Hungry Hungry Hippos, Jenga, Lincoln Logs, Lite Brite, and My Little Pony.

Toys, as in art such as sculpture, have size and weight, test limits, stimulate the senses, and invite interest and interaction. When toys respond as children create with them in an open-ended way, the movement reflects the dynamic of artistic discovery. Children need to take time to balance learning at school with fun and relaxation at home, and creative play covers dramatic, social and artistic development.

Not everything a child does has to be 'significant'. Doodling is fun and relaxing. Sketching is an important process, is relaxing, and prepares for more serious work. Creating something new from a cardboard box, a stick, or other elements commonly found in the environment, is also considered valuable play.

It is hard to put a price on the value of these experiences; as in any field of art, they are very subjective. The world of toys and play continues to create a blend of art, science, technology, design and child development, as the crucible of play is shaped not only for the child, but also for parents, grandparents, and everyone else who recognises the essential benefits involved in play, and values playfulness for all ages. We must provide a wide range of opportunities for diversified play. For the future, let us try to maintain a balance as well as a full range of strong hues, colours and shapes on our rich palette of play. Selectivity, challenge, and creativity should be among our goals to give children every opportunity to use their imaginations. That is one of the greatest gifts anyone can offer.

Dr. Toy™, **Stevanne Auerbach**, PhD, has been for many years one of the leading professionals on children's play, educational toys and related products. Dr. Auerbach relies on forty-five plus years of training and hands-on experience to select the best educationally oriented, skill-building products for her annual award programs. Her book *Dr. Toy's Smart Play/Smart Toys: How to Select and Use the Best*, now it its fourth edition, has been published in thirteen countries.

www.drtoy.com

Acknowledgements

Sheila Armstrong, Dr Stevanne
Auerbach, Melanie Bradley, Dáire
Convery, Uaneen Convery, Carole
Craig, Lisa Dooey, James Dugan,
Meghan Elward-Duffy, Gráinne Evans,
Kevin Fox, Ruben James, Alexandra
Karakas, Elaine Malone, Danny
O'Reilly, Paul Oates, Caroline Sullivan.

Our thanks also to those companies
whose products are included.
Every effort has been made to trace
copyright holders and to obtain their
permission for the use of copyright
material. The publisher apologises
for any errors or omissions in the
list overleaf and would be grateful if
notified of any corrections that should
be incorporated in future reprints or
editions of this book.